P9-CKR-596

XOXO,
CODY

Rigsby, Cody,
XOXO, Cody / an opinionated
homosexual's guide to self-lov
[2023]
33305255944484
ca   10/10/23

XOXO,
CODY

An Opinionated Homosexual's Guide to Self-Love, Relationships, and Tactful Pettiness

Cody Rigsby

with Rachel Bertsche

BALLANTINE BOOKS

NEW YORK

This is a work of nonfiction. Some names and identifying details have been changed.

Copyright © 2023 by Cody Rigsby

All rights reserved.

Published in the United States by Ballantine Books,
an imprint of Random House,
a division of Penguin Random House LLC, New York.

BALLANTINE is a registered trademark and the colophon
is a trademark of Penguin Random House LLC.

LIBRARY OF CONGRESS CATALOGING-IN-PUBLICATION DATA
Names: Rigsby, Cody, author.
Title: XOXO, Cody / an opinionated homosexual's guide to self-love,
relationships, and tactful pettiness / Cody Rigsby.
Other titles: Hugs and kisses, Cody
Description: First edition. | New York: Ballantine Books, [2023] |
Identifiers: LCCN 2023010922 (print) | LCCN 2023010923 (ebook) |
ISBN 9780593722534 (hardcover) | ISBN 9780593722541 (ebook)
Subjects: LCSH: Personal trainers—United States—Biography. |
Gay men—United States—Social conditions. | Self-love (Psychology)—
United States. | Peloton. | Dancing with the stars (Television program) |
Male dancers—United States—Biography.
Classification: LCC GV331.R54 A3 2023 (print) | LCC GV331.R54
(ebook) | DDC 613.7/1092 [B]—dc23/eng/20230310
LC record available at https://lccn.loc.gov/2023010922
LC ebook record available at https://lccn.loc.gov/2023010923

PRINTED IN THE UNITED STATES OF AMERICA ON ACID-FREE PAPER

randomhousebooks.com

2 4 6 8 9 7 5 3 1

First Edition

Dedicated to our dear lord and savior,
Britney Jean Spears.
Without your gyrating hips
and diamond-encrusted G-strings,
I wouldn't be the man I am today.

Introduction

I have a lot of opinions. Kevin is the hottest Backstreet Boy. Grape jelly is a crime against nature. A threesome will never—never!—save your relationship. Same goes for a baby. If you wear flip-flops in New York City, you do not love yourself.

But if there is one opinion—no, one TRUTH—that I hold above all others, it's that we shouldn't take ourselves, or our lives, too seriously. And that we shouldn't let the fear of looking stupid or messing up or being judged hold us back from living the lives we deserve. It's not that deep, boo.

Life can be scary. I know this. But I also know that facing the scary shit, even sometimes laughing *in* the face of it, can change our lives. When I first auditioned to be a Peloton instructor, I had never taught a fitness class. I was fumbling through my twenties, trying to keep my head above water. I worked as a cater waiter by day, and in the evenings I helped the bottle service girls at the Box, a provocative nightclub on the Lower East Side, making sure no one was taking videos of the topless performers. (Shaking titties has been a theme of my career.) Hustling until three A.M. was bearable only because I got to watch a trans performance artist pee all over wealthy investment bankers.

Earlier in my career, I'd tried to make it as a professional dancer. I performed with a bunch of big names, including Nicki Minaj and Katy Perry, but by the time I was at the Box, dancing was mostly behind me. Still, one of the directors there had a friend who worked at an early-stage fitness company, and he was looking for performers who were interested in exercise and who might be good at teaching. That director knew I was a dancer, and he knew I liked to go to the gym, so he sent me the listing. And even though I hadn't taught fitness a day in my life, even though I was scared I might be in over my head, I thought, *why not make a little extra coin?* No, I didn't know what I was doing. Yes, I knew I might look like a fool. But I sent in my headshot and résumé anyway, and after a thirty-minute interview, Marion Roaman, then the chief content officer of Peloton, announced, "You start training next week."

What can I say, a cute face and determination can open a lot of doors.

A year later, I was working at Peloton full-time. Nine years after that, I'm still at the company, teaching cycling and boot camp and dance cardio and meditation classes to seven million members, and I've taken my fun and flirty approach to fitness to a global platform, including an appearance on *Dancing with the Stars* and a hosting gig at the GLAAD Media Awards.

It's been a wild ride, but it hasn't been an easy one. When I got the job at Peloton, I was in the ring alongside people like Robin Arzón, badass lawyer and ultramarathoner, and I was just trying to figure out how to teach a class while also pedaling my legs. When I was cast on *Dancing with the Stars*, I was competing against icons like Mel C., aka Sporty Spice, aka the hardest-working Spice Girl (this is not up for debate; she can do a back handspring and handle the most challenging vocals), and it was terrifying! And then I got COVID and had to dance alone via Zoom from my apartment . . . ON NATIONAL TELEVISION. (And to Britney Spears no less. If there's one thing you should know about me, it's that Britney is my queen—and has been ever since sixth grade, when they projected the ". . . Baby One More Time" video onto a screen at the Guilford Middle School dance. I was immediately enthralled. Like, *Werk, what is this, I love it.* Whenever I hear Britney Spears, I fuck shit up, and it's not so easy to fuck shit up over Zoom.) Every time I do something new or out of my comfort zone—which happens more and more these days—I get nervous. The world is a crazy place, and there's a lot going on that is out of our control. Sometimes you need to fix your tits and get on with it, and other times you have to sit in the uncomfortable spaces to get through them. But when we can recognize the absurdity of it all and laugh about it together, it doesn't feel so tough. So laugh, bitch! Laugh at it all! Adding levity to the difficult moments is what connects us to our joy—and there's enough out there trying to steal our joy (hello, Jamie Lynn Spears).

Here's something else I've been known to tell riders, in between my TED Talks on topics like black licorice (no), *TRL* (YES), and cash bars (why did you invite me?): You are fierce. You are fabulous. You are a hot steaming plate of fajitas at a packed Chili's on a Friday night turning heads.

No, not the complimentary basket of chips and salsa—you're the fajita! The shrimp fajitas. The expensive kind. That's the kind of confidence I'm looking for from you. Rich shrimp-fajita-level confidence. Because before you can get fit, before you can get paid, before you can find somebody to love who will love you like you deserve, you need to love yourself.

Listen, I don't really know how to say this without sounding like a cringey asshole, but here goes: I always knew I was a star. I knew I was special, even when I was being told that everything about who I was was wrong. And that negativity came at me a lot. As a kid, I got made fun of for acting like a girl. I got ridiculed for loving to dance. I was the boy in seventh grade teaching the girls the "Oops! . . . I Did It Again" choreography. (You know those filler days at the end of the year when testing is over but summer break hasn't started yet? By the end of those two days in the year 2000 every thirteen-year-old girl in my class knew how to move like Britney in her red vinyl catsuit.) Not exactly under the radar. Even as an out gay man, I felt pressure to play the part of the hyper-masculine gay guy—a role that is very not me—because that's what lots of men gravitate to. But even when I *was* trying to hide my authentic self, or change myself to fit a mold, I believed, deep down, that one day I would shine. As a kid I thought I would be an actor, because that's what stars did. Then, when I realized I couldn't act, I thought I'd be a dancer—and I had some success there, but plenty of failures, too. It wasn't until I landed at Peloton and was finally being validated for being GAY AS FUCK that I could look back and say, *See, bitch, you always knew you were a star. People tried to convince you that you weren't worthy, that you were extra, that you needed to be different . . . but you had it all along.*

That said, feeling destined for stardom and loving yourself are not the same thing. Even if loving other people comes naturally, it's hard to hold the mirror up to ourselves and face all the insecurities and messiness of our lives and still remember that we're that bitch. For me, that aha moment came after a breakup. I'd been dating a guy that I loved a lot, and the relationship ended because I cheated on him—well, there was some gray area based on what we'd agreed upon, but I definitely hurt this person that I cared about, and I realized I had some real work to do. I understood that if I could sabotage my own happiness so severely, if I could get in my own way like that, then I needed to focus on loving myself. That's when I began to connect to the idea of self-love, to prioritize it for myself, and start encouraging it in others.

So, a lot of this book will touch on just that: how to love yourself. Because it can be confusing! Self-love doesn't mean never being sad or not having a hard time. It means valuing yourself enough to feel those feelings while still knowing your worth. And it means pressing pause on the wallowing long enough to take care of yourself in the ways that you need. I often define self-love as the act of differentiating between what you need and what you want. Sometimes you want a rest day, but sometimes you truly *need* a rest day. Sometimes you want another vodka soda, but what you actually need is a gallon of H_2O. You might *want* a hot guy with tattoos that leaves you on "read" for twelve hours and then gives you a one-word answer, but what you *need* is a nice guy with a good job who talks to his mom once a week. And while you're reading this book, learning for yourself the difference between what you want and what you need? Well, I'm not saying I'll fill in any gaps by *telling* you what you need, but I *am* here to say that nobody, for example, needs a wooden LIVE LAUGH LOVE sign from Home Goods in their living room. They just don't. It's time to elevate your décor. You're welcome, Susan.

Which brings me back to the beginning of this introduction, and all those opinions I mentioned. I've had them all my life. I was an energetic and talkative little boy who turned into a brash and up-front man. It has gotten me into trouble, I'm not gonna lie. But I'm an opinionated homosexual, I can't help it. When it comes to my takes on pop culture or modern-day behavior, those observations may sound like judgments, but I prefer the term *tactful pettiness.* I may be reading someone for filth, but I like to think I do so with respect and consideration even in my bitchiest moments. Shade is rooted in respect. If I'm not reading you, I don't love you. And when it comes to giving advice . . . well, I do keep it real, but, like I said, it always comes from a place of love. I just want people to be better. I want to share what I've learned in case I can protect you from making the same mistakes I have. And maybe it's because I'm a good listener, or maybe it's just that I love to hear myself talk, but something about that honest-to-a-fault approach seems to work, because my friends have been coming to me for advice for as long as I can remember.

Since early 2020, Peloton users have gotten in on the fun, sending me their relationship, self-love, and pop culture questions for a recurring series called "XOXO, Cody." During the rides, I've answered questions ranging from

"What should I do about a boyfriend who only says 'I love you' when he's drunk?" (Have a conversation! Communicate!) to "Should I pursue my work crush at the holiday party?" (Have you not seen *Love Actually*? It didn't work for Laura Linney.) From "How many dates should I wait to have sex?" (Um, zero to however many you want) to "My booty call doesn't even get me off, what should I do?" (You did not survive a pandemic to fake an orgasm, okay?) I've shared stories from my own relationships, and sounded off, more than once, on which Disney princes I'd love to smash (Beast, but only in Beast form; he was too pretty as a man).

So that's what I hope to do with this book. To share the life lessons I've learned in my thirty-six years, in case they can help you become the best or most joyful version of yourself. You don't have to be a Peloton member or a fitness junkie to get something out of these pages; you just have to be willing to laugh and to consider the idea that life doesn't have to be so heavy all the time. I'll tell you stories of my childhood growing up in North Carolina; of the drunken night in college I couldn't get it up for a girl and finally accepted, once and for all, that I had sugar in my tank; of moving to New York to do an internship at Broadway Dance Center; of transplanting my mama Cindy to Brooklyn, four blocks away from me, and finally making peace with our relationship. I'll offer my take on raising your fee (the time is now!), and share what it was really like to dance with the stars. As with any "XOXO, Cody" affair, I'll answer some of your questions, taken straight from my DMs, and I'll detail my personal opinions on everything from the best after-school snacks to the most frightening *Mario Kart* characters.

(If you choose to be Princess Peach, we have some daddy issues to process, babe.)

My hope for you is that, after laughing with me for a couple hundred pages, you put down this book and feel more empowered to laugh at *yourself*. The reality is we're all just sitting here on a rock in a solar system inside another solar system and we don't know shit about what else is out there. We. Don't. Know. Shit! Hell, this might just be a simulation. When we remember that, it's a lot easier to say, "Okay, whatever, Imma try to do what I want and if it sticks, great. And if I fail, I'll pick myself up, dust off my wig, and keep pumping."

There's one last thing I want you to know as you embark upon these pages: I'm figuring shit out right alongside you. I am a work in progress. I have days where I feel like I've got my shit together—I drink my water and do my workouts and feel like I'm conquering the world one cringe TikTok post at a time—and I have days where I feel like a trashy bitch, staying in my underwear all day, bingeing *Golden Girls* and drinking white wine with frozen grapes (to keep it chilled, of course). That's okay. The idea is not to be perfect. The idea is to be yourself.

So fix your wig. Grab a water. Grab a towel. Get your life together.

Let's do this.

XOXO,
CODY

CHAPTER ONE

Growing Up Cody

I was born in California and lived, until I was eight, in Burbank. If you're not familiar with L.A., here's the quick rundown: Burbank is in the Valley, and it's largely known for being the home of production studios like Warner Bros. and the Walt Disney Studios. For much of my young life I was obsessed with the idea of being an actor—not necessarily because I was good at it (I was fine) but because I found fame and notoriety incredibly enticing. I don't know if that dream was a direct result of my childhood proximity to Hollywood, but the entertainment business was in my orbit and likely influenced my thinking. And I looked the part, too. I had super-blond hair, tan skin . . . it was all very Zack Morris. My favorite childhood picture is of me rocking a neon pink Mickey Mouse shirt with cutoff sleeves. With the Disneyland vibe and yellow locks and the sun-kissed skin, I was serving serious California Boy realness.

All that said, my childhood was not exactly what you might picture when I invoke Bayside High and Hollywood and the entertainment industry. Namely, we were broke. My mom worked various odd jobs but she had trouble holding them, and none paid especially well. The two of us lived in a one-bedroom apartment on the first floor of an apartment complex. It was just the two us—my father died when I was four months old. He and my mom were both addicts, and he died of a drug overdose, though my mom always told me he died of a heart attack. That's probably true if we want to get into semantics, but it's not the full picture. I didn't learn the truth until I was twelve or thirteen, when I was going through boxes of old papers and came across my dad's death certificate, which listed drug overdose as the cause of death.

I don't remember my dad, obviously, and don't really feel any connection to him at this point—he and my mother weren't married, so I don't even use his last name. And good thing, because otherwise I'd be Cody Brudnicki, which is fine, I guess, but it certainly doesn't have that Cody Rigsby ring to it.

My memories of living in California are a little spotty, but good or bad they all center around one person: my mom. Cindy and I were quite a pair. I didn't have any siblings, and my mother always made a point to tell me that she was never sure if she even wanted kids. She had me at thirty-three and she'd definitely had a few abortions before that. She's told me multiple times, "Cody, you were the one I kept." She's always had a way with words, that Cindy.

There was a lot of joy and spontaneity and silliness during those L.A. years—the fun of my mom and me blasting *The Bodyguard* soundtrack in the car on the way to school, or making sun tea on our patio (You know sun tea, right? Instead of tea bags in boiling water, you put them in regular water and leave the whole jug outside in the California heat.

Hours later—voilà!—you've got gallons of tea for a cute summer refreshment. A science experiment!), or riding up the Pacific Coast Highway to see my grandmother in Santa Barbara. She lived there with her husband/my mom's step-dad, Charles, who we all called Dickie. I thought that was hilarious because, well, I was seven. Dickie had a prosthetic leg, and for that fact alone I found him fascinating because, again, seven.

At home, my mom and I were roommates—we lived in a one-bedroom but the bedroom was big. She slept on one side and I slept against the opposite wall in a lofted bed, above a desk. We lived in that bedroom during the 1994 Northridge earthquake, a 6.7 magnitude early-morning quake centered in the Valley. It was terrifying. I woke up to the literal earth shaking! I was groggy and confused and in my stupor/terror I couldn't figure out how to get out of my five-feet-off-the-ground bed, so my mom *broke off* the guardrail to get me out. I guess it was that maternal-strength-survival-instinct you always hear about—you know how they say a mom can lift a car when her kid's in danger?—because this bitch legit ripped off the side of my bed and picked me up and made me stand in the doorway to the bathroom. Back then we were all taught that the safest place to stand in an earthquake was under a doorframe. Turns out that was fake news, but it's a myth we were all buying in the '90s. So anyway, I'm standing in the doorway, having just woken up, and like any kid suddenly awake in the middle of the night, I had to pee. My mom let me go to the bathroom, which probably wasn't the smartest decision because the bathroom was home to many shelves of glass perfume bottles. There I was, standing at the toilet, the earth shaking beneath my feet and perfume bottles falling to the ground and shattering around me as I tried to pee. It was traumatic.

After the earthquake, the entire apartment complex community looked out for each other and took care of one another. We were literally shook, and we hung out in the shared courtyard most of the next day because it was dangerous to be inside. People were grilling and making food for one another, and it was one of the first times I remember seeing a community really come together. The neighbor kids were my closest friends—I was the only white kid in the complex; it was mostly Latino families. I was invited to so many birthday parties and celebrations that my memories of that time almost all involve piñatas and barbecues and this amazing birthday cake that I still think of to this day. It was a tres leches cake with strawberries and almonds in the middle, with this light and airy whipped cream–type frosting. Perfection.

As much fun as my mom and I had during those California days, there was also some real darkness. While I didn't explicitly understand that my mom was a drug addict, there were moments when I knew something was not right. When I was six, my mother put me in the back seat of her car one evening and drove along a bunch of poorly lit streets into a sketchy neighborhood, where we came to a stop at an underpass. A thin man who was missing a few teeth approached her window. I couldn't understand why we would talk to this guy, but the next thing I knew my mother was rolling down her window and handing over cash. In return, he pulled two balloons out of his mouth and gave them to her. Looking back, it's obvious that she was buying heroin, but all I knew at the time was that something felt weird and unsafe. I couldn't make sense of what I was seeing, and I tried to push aside any inkling that something was off, because I loved my mom and didn't want to believe that she would put me in danger. Still, it was not right, nor was it okay (thank you, Whitney).

My mom also had these friends, Winnie and Trey, who she hung out with a lot. I liked spending time with the three of them because I was a kid who wanted attention and wanted to be a part of things (some might say I'm an adult who wants attention and to be a part of things, but that's a conversation for another day). When we went to their houses, my mom and Winnie would disappear into the bathroom for a long time. Like, a really long time. Back then I was just like, *What the fuck is happening?*, but of course now I know. Ding! They were doing drugs! With me in the next room! I was even there the day Winnie's boyfriend died—probably, I know now, of an overdose. While I was too young to articulate or fully understand what was going on, I knew there was something desperate and scary about the way we lived.

Toward the end of second grade, my mom announced that it was time to move. She told me it was because I was getting older and she didn't want me to grow up in Los Angeles— she wanted a simpler life for us, she said—though I imagine that some of the motive for moving across the country, away from her family and the only home she'd ever known, was to escape access to drugs.

She made me a proposal: We were going to move, but I got to choose where. The options were Denver, where my grandfather lived; Scottsdale, Arizona, where one of her good friends lived; or North Carolina, where another of her good friends lived and where a friend of mine from school had moved a few years earlier. The fact that she was asking an eight-year-old to make the call . . . well, I guess we can see where I get my indecisiveness from. Surprise, I chose the city where my friend lived, so by early summer we were packing up to head east.

My mom and I put all our shit in a moving van and crawled into our blue Chrysler with our three cats and two dogs for the road trip of a lifetime. We were like Oprah and Gayle heading across the country, if Gayle were a gay eight-year-old who loved Ace of Base and Oprah traded her bread addiction for something heavier. We took our sweet time getting across the country. It was the first time I had left the state of California, and we were in no rush. We stopped for visits in Arizona and Colorado, but the pinnacle of the journey was in Kansas. By that point the Chrysler's air-conditioning had broken, and it was *hot*. It was so fucking hot that we had to open the cat carriers. So we're driving down the highway with the windows open—we weren't trying to die of heat and we weren't trying to kill these animals—when I look in my rearview mirror, and there is my cat, Ruby, resting her head out of the windowsill, try-ing to get cool. Then, just as I turn to look back at her, she legit jumps—no, leaps!—out of the window. It was like a scene in slow-motion—Ruby vaulted out of the car, hit the median on the grass, rolled over, and then just kept pump-ing. Kitty said *Fuck it, I can't take it anymore,* and my mom and I still talk about it to this day. The gag is, her name was Ruby, it happened in Kansas . . . it was giving *Wizard of Oz.*

My mom did circle back and try to find her, but no luck. I always imagine Ruby found a nice farm to live on.

Making our way from California to North Carolina took two weeks, and as we inched toward our final destination—Stokes County, North Carolina—let me tell you, the vibes were far from immaculate. "We're twenty minutes away!" my mom told me as we neared her friend Glenda's house, where we'd be staying before we settled into our own place. I took one look out the window and burst into tears. There were no sidewalks. The road was . . . not exactly gravel, but it was bumpy. Unrefined. I looked at my mother, horrified. "Where am I going to rollerblade?" I asked. Selfish-ass kid, I know, but this was 1995! Rollerblading was rad.

We only stayed in Stokes County for one year. It was the fucking boonies of North Carolina. My third-grade class had not a single person of color. It was white people as far as the eye could see, and I thought that was fucking bizarre. I'd come from California where, yes, my neighbors were all Latino, but my friends were also Black and Asian. I was used to diversity and this was . . . not it. It was serious culture shock. Luckily my mom felt the same way, because after a year we moved another forty miles to Greensboro, which was super segregated and fucked up in its own way, but at least had some diversity. And it had sidewalks to rollerblade.

If my memories of California all have a sort of Cody-and-Cindy buddy comedy vibe, life as a kid in North Carolina felt more like a solo act. My mom worked a lot—she took catering jobs at the local country club, worked at the Greensboro Coliseum, and waited tables—which meant I spent a lot of time at home alone. I'd have to fend for myself after school, either cooking ramen noodles or eating what my mom left out for me. It could get pretty lonely. We lived in a two-bedroom apartment at that point, an upgrade from California because we each had our own space, but it did not feel like a home. My friends in Greensboro mostly came from nuclear families and lived in nicely decorated houses, and ours was anything but. I specifically hated our living room, if you could call it that. There was no couch, just a bunch of boxes in piles and a carpet that smelled like dog piss because we had three dogs. Yes, I had my own room, which had a box spring mattress, a TV and VCR, a built-in desk, and some toys and books, but mostly the space felt dirty and unsettled.

The Greensboro living situation affected me in two seemingly opposite ways: I was ashamed and embarrassed by our dirty home and my lack of a conventional family, but I also had a strong desire for attention from others, because my home life was pretty damn lonely. I didn't give much thought, back in California, to the fact that my dad wasn't around. I knew plenty of kids being raised by single moms, and there were all sorts of different family dynamics in our apartment complex. But in Greensboro, it was a lot of mom-dad-sister-brother shit. I felt like I was different, or weird, or pathetic, because my father wasn't there. You know that feeling when you break up with someone and you don't really miss *them* but instead you miss the *feeling* of them? When it's far less about the actual person than it is about the comfort that comes with having a partner? That's how I felt about my father. I idealized the concept of him, but I didn't actually know much about the man himself. My mom and I almost never talked about him. I knew I looked a lot like him—I've seen pictures of him as a kid and it's like looking at my childhood self—and every now and then I'd do something that would make my mother say, "Oh, that reminds me of your father," but that was pretty much the extent of it.

The truth is, I probably dodged a bullet. My father's passing was certainly tragic. He was in his forties when he died, and that's too young to go. And I feel for my mother, who was only thirty-three at the time. She lost a man she loved and the father of her son. She had to raise a kid alone, and that must have been scary and lonely. But for me, what I missed most was the sense of security that I thought came with having a nuclear family. I was embarrassed by the instability of my home life as compared to my friends' seemingly very stable and secure family structures.

My best friend was a boy named Justin. His family owned a shoe business, and they had a big and beautifully decorated home—his bedroom was their entire basement— and also a beach house. His house was clean and homey, and, honestly, it fucked with my head. I mean, we were poor. Like, scrounging-in-the-couch-for-enough-change-to-get-2-for-$2-Big-Macs poor. And as much as my mom tried to shield me from the desperation of those times, any kid can recognize the lack of security. You learn to fear it, and to feel ashamed of it.

Despite not wanting to call attention to what I was beginning to realize was a pretty unstable upbringing, I was also embracing the part of myself that was all about clowning around and being talkative and generally giving off very big energy. Justin and I were constantly goofing off in class, distracting other kids, and doing stupid shit like reading the thesaurus aloud in study hall. I was a performer. I was in show choir, and I played Kenickie in the high school production of *Grease* (perhaps you saw the photo of T-Bird Cody during *Grease* week on *Dancing with the Stars*).

No one has ever accused Cody Wyatt Rigsby of being a nerdy-ass wallflower, but at times my outgoing and social nature, or my desire to make people laugh, felt more like a survival tactic than a personality trait. I craved company and acceptance. I wanted to get attention because I wasn't getting a lot of it at home. I didn't want to feel alone, and I didn't want to feel afraid. And this was especially true in a world where the word *gay* was tossed around as the ultimate insult. I hadn't necessarily come to terms with my own sexuality in elementary school or middle school, but I knew that my high-energy, talking-a-mile-a-minute nature struck some people as girly, and I didn't want to be an outcast. This was the *TRL* era. The boys around me were listening to Limp Bizkit or rap music or toxic masculinity rock, and I was blasting Britney and the Spice Girls. I was into pop music and dancing, and there were some people who said that was wrong. But I couldn't fight who I was. I couldn't hide it, and I didn't want to. So I was lucky that I was a natural extrovert with an instinctive ability to crack a joke and win over a crowd. It defined me, but it also protected me.

Life in Greensboro continued pretty much at that clip until I turned sixteen. I like to describe my upbringing as "not completely traumatizing," which, sad to say, feels like a win. Sure, I got made fun of for my cheap clothes, which was upsetting, and I had crushes on boys, which was confusing, but I was unabashedly myself because even then I knew that myself was pretty damn fierce. My future im-

proved dramatically on my sixteenth birthday, though, because that was the day I turned in my application to work at
McDonald's, and with employment came independence.

My work ethic developed early. I wanted security and
stability, and, shit, I wanted to be able to buy things without
a constant scramble, so as soon as I could work, I did. My
first job was at a pizza shop fifteen minutes from my house.
I worked under the table handing out flyers for five dollars
an hour. The manager would drive me to this nice suburban
neighborhood, drop me off on a street corner, and pick me
up three hours later. I didn't have a cellphone, so I just had
to wait and hope he came back for me. It was a different
time, y'all. But literally on the day I turned sixteen, I showed
up at the McDonald's on High Point Road with my application, ready to work. Of course she was turning it, so they
put me in the drive-thru—they only put the fierce girls in
the drive-thru, because that's where the money is made, and
those girls have to be quick. I was clawing my way up the
McDonald's corporate ladder. Soon I got my second job at
Steak 'n Shake, and that was a great gig because I was waiting tables. I was making ten to fifteen dollars an hour which,
for a sixteen-year-old in Greensboro, North Carolina, is a
lot of money!

I bought my first car with my earnings from
McDonald's—a black Kia Sephia with roll-up windows that
I got for $1,600 at auction. I even saved up enough to put in
a CD player and new speakers. Of course, my mom ended
up using the car a lot, because she didn't have one of her
own. (By then the blue Chrysler had gone up in flames, literally. One day during our first year in North Carolina my
mom was driving to work and something went wrong with

the engine, so she pulled over and got out and suddenly the car burst into flames. I kid you not.) But having my own transportation gave me enough freedom to score some independence and grow into myself a little bit. And that started with my clothes.

Back then, everyone was wearing Abercrombie and American Eagle, and I did not want to be that girl. My girlfriend Kacie and I would drive an hour and a half to the Urban Outfitters in Charlotte, and we really felt like we were doing something because they had more unique and stylish offerings. My classmates would show up to school wearing the same Abercrombie polo shirt, while I was rocking my THE POPE IS DOPE baby blue tee and distressed denim. Turns out we *were* doing something, because come senior year we were both voted best dressed. In our yearbook it was called "Style of Their Own," but, babe, we were the best dressed.

I made high school work, and I carved out a niche for myself, but I never felt completely at home. Any good memories are overshadowed by the insecurity that accompanied an unpredictable and unstable upbringing, which was compounded by a confusion—or shame—about my sexuality.

Kacie and I are still friends all these years later. She still lives in North Carolina, and at this point, she's the only reason I go back. I left Greensboro after college, and while I've returned to North Carolina a couple of times—to help my mom pack up to move, and for Kacie's wedding (and I'll go again to meet her baby and be her guncle)—there's really nothing else for me there anymore.

Though I do crave Bojangles and Cook Out, North Carolina's finest fast-food establishments.

CHAPTER TWO

I'm Coming Out

In seventh grade, I became friends with a girl named Jenna Barnhardt. Like any good little Christian girl in our good little Southern city, Jenna was active in the church community. She came from a religious household, and church was a cornerstone of her family life, so Jenna invited all her non-churchgoing friends to give religion a spin. I started joining her for Wednesday night Bible study because, first of all, they served food beforehand, including the best potato casserole that I've ever had to this day. Those church ladies slayed that casserole. It had broken Wavy Lay's potato chips on top, and I thought it was all that and bag of chips. (I'll never pass up an opportunity to use my '90s slang, or to make a pun.) But also, Bible study was social. There were teens and tweens my age, and we'd play games and hang out. I was into the friendship aspect of it, and the sense of community it offered, and as time went on church started to feel more like home. It helped that Jenna's family began to take me under their wing. They'd pick me up on Wednesdays for Bible study, or on Sunday mornings for church, and then we'd all go to lunch afterward. Jenna's family offered stability, and they were extremely kind people. Spending time with them was an outlet, an escape from an insecure home life.

Of course, as a person continues to go to church and Bible study, it becomes more than fun and games and potato casserole. You start to become indoctrinated, and I was no exception. There was this lock-in event one weekend—essentially a chaperoned group sleepover at the church—which started with a long sermon and ended with the pastor asking everyone to accept Jesus into their hearts. I found the whole thing pretty weird, but they scared me enough to believe I would go to hell if I didn't buy in, so by the time I reached high school, I was squarely in my God phase. In fact, there came a time when I was so religious that I was certain my mom was going to hell—she had *not* accepted Jesus into her heart—so I tried to evangelize to her and save her and she was just like, *Boo, that's not happening.* "Religion is not for me," she said. "If you want to get into that, congratulations, but I'll pass. No thank you." Meanwhile, teenage Cody was sitting over here like, "You're going to hell! Accept Jesus! Go to church!"

She was not into it.

At the same time as I was establishing myself as part of the church community, I was also starting to grapple with puberty and hormones and having more sexual thoughts and desires . . . but I was having them about boys. From the age of five I was curious about other boys' bodies—in California my neighbor and I used to play swordfight, the naked kind—and by middle school I started having real crushes on boys. For a long time I had a thing for this kid Jared, who was actually a complete asshole to me and would make fun of my imitation brand-name shoes. (I think he's the reason

I'm now obsessed with sneakers.) I couldn't have articulated "I have a crush on Jared" back then, but did I go home after school and masturbate to thoughts of him? Yes. Also AC Slater. And Mark Wahlberg. We were too poor for a computer back then, which meant no internet porn, so I would go to the public library and print out pictures of Marky Mark in his underwear to bring home for my viewing pleasure.

And yet, at Guilford Baptist Church in the year 2000? They weren't about that life. I was going through a whole mess of emotions: There was the comfort of being welcomed by Jenna's family and seemingly accepted into the church, but there was also a lot of guilt. I worried that I was going to hell, that something was wrong with me, that I had to change who I was. Consider how many times a thirteen-to-sixteen-year-old boy thinks about sex. It's *a lot.* And now imagine that every time you think about sex you're also thinking about how wrong your feelings are, and feeling guilty about desires you can't control. It was a constant internal battle, this religious confusion, and it caused a lot of stress and anxiety and, I know now, trauma. Not to mention that I was a middle schooler in the South, where kids were constantly making fun of gay people and throwing the word "faggot" around. It was a lot to deal with, and my solution, for a little while at least, was to try to pray the gay away.

Luckily, my desire to make money outweighed my devotion to the church, so as soon as I got the job at McDonald's and had to work on Wednesday nights or Sunday mornings, my religious fervor began to fade. I started making new friends, and owning my own car meant I could be a bit more self-reliant. And as I came into my own, I started questioning the teachings of the church from a rational standpoint. I wasn't out yet, but I knew I was attracted to boys. I was smart enough, at the very least, to distance myself from a religion that told me my very being was wrong.

Let us not forget, this was the South at the turn of the millennium. I was not ready to be out and proud, both because I was still coming to terms with my own feelings and because, frankly, I was scared. I was scared of being othered and of being made fun of, and I was also scared of violence, though I'm not sure I fully understood that at the time. I was in high school from 2001 to 2005. Matthew Shepard, the college student in Wyoming who was beaten to death for being gay, was killed in 1998. It was impossible not to clock that underlying threat.

Even in my own home, I worried about being accepted. My mom considered herself super progressive. She'd had gay friends my whole life. When we lived in L.A., she took me to this hairstylist named Pat, who had a husband and presented as a woman but had this different, sort of deep, voice. One day, when I was in my twenties and had just started learning more about trans people, I asked my mom about her. "Mom, remember Pat?" I said. "Was she trans?"

My mom's response, more or less, was "DUH."

But when people think they're in a safe space to be homophobic—even people who think they're accepting or tolerant—they make offhand jokes or commit microaggressions that they don't even think about. If you're a kid that thinks he might be gay? You absolutely notice. One day, my mom and I were at a discount bath store buying towels, and

I picked out a set I thought would be good. "What about these?" I said, holding up my towels of choice.

"Those are pretty gay," she said.

Each time she made a comment like that, and she made them more than once, it planted another seed of doubt.

Back then, I didn't want to be gay. I knew that the "normal" way of life was straight, and I wanted to be a part of that. It's not like no one ever wondered if I was gay. I didn't have girlfriends, except for one poor girl for a few weeks in middle school. She was my first kiss, and it was incredibly uncomfortable, since every time our lips touched it felt like a giant lie. Girls in high school would ask, "Are you gay or not?" They'd say, "If you're not gay then kiss me." So, okay, I'd make out with them and that would shut them up, which was . . . weird.

Then, one day during the summer between my junior and senior years of high school, I was at the mall with Kacie, debating a fuchsia collared shirt from Express, when I locked eyes with a blond-haired blue-eyed boy with a rocking body and a really nice ass. It had all the vibes of a sexy meet-cute rom-com moment. You know, very *She spotted him across the room and next thing she knew they were going at it in a bathroom stall.* Except in this case we had all the googly eyes with none of the steamy bathroom sex. I watched as he paid for a bunch of clothes at the front register, and as he left, he turned and gave me one last look. It might have ended there except later, as Kacie headed into Wet Seal, I spotted the mystery boy heading up the escalator.

"I'm going to go check out the video game store," I told

Kacie. As soon as I was out of her eyesight, I beelined to the escalator.

As I ascended into the food court, there he was, sitting alone at a two top. We exchanged looks again, but this time we didn't break eye contact. I find it interesting, even to this day, how without even saying anything two people can know they're both gay and that they are into each other.

"I'm not out, so keep this between us," I said as I slid into the seat across the table from him.

Those were the first words I said to my first-ever boyfriend. It was scary and risky, but I was ready for my turn at romance.

We talked for a while. His name was Nolan, and he was a year older than me. He was a cheerleader and was going to UNC Greensboro that fall, and even though he was already out, he was super respectful and understanding of the fact that I was not.

By the time I left the mall, his phone number was in my pocket.

For our first date, Nolan and I went for a walk in a local park. If anyone saw us it would have been easy enough to explain, but I was still nervous. It wasn't just the fear that I would get found out. The simple fact that I was walking next to a boy, and knowing I was on a date, had my insides buzzing. Eventually we made our way off the beaten path and into the woods of the park so that no one could see us. And there, during the summer before my senior year of high school, I had my first gay kiss.

It felt incredible. I'd kissed plenty of girls by that point, and it was always uncomfortable, so the feeling of touching someone else in a way that felt good and right? It was such a relief.

Nolan and I dated that whole summer, but by the time my senior year started, we agreed to break up. He was going off to college and didn't want a high school boyfriend, and I'd realized that I couldn't be in a relationship while I was still in hiding. As much fun as we were having, I wasn't ready to come out.

Then, one day, during the first weeks of senior year, I was sitting in English class when this girl Brette walked in. Brette was a cheerleader, and she must have known Nolan from the cheer world because after getting settled in her seat, she turned to me and said, "Hey, Cody, I didn't know you knew my friend Nolan."

WHAT?! Oh fuck. Did this motherfucker out me?!

My heart stopped. I was super uncomfortable, but just sort of smiled, mumbling something generally incoherent, and Brette went on. "Yeah, he told me you guys were friends." I let out a huge sigh of relief. My secret was safe.

Moments like that one—where I felt *this close* to being outed—occurred, if not frequently, then at least with some regularity in the early 2000s. The most memorable was in the fall of my freshman year of college. I went to UNC Greensboro and was rooming with Justin, my best friend from high school, and one Friday night we went to another friend's dorm room to hang out and drink cheap vodka, as one does at age eighteen. There was a visitor there, someone's friend from high school (who was still in high school herself), and this girl set her sights on me immediately. She was flirting, laughing at my jokes, lightly grazing my arm in that way that could only mean one thing, and somehow we made it to my friend's top bunk and started making out.

"Should we go back to your place?" she asked.

"Sure," I said, because I assumed that's what a straight guy would say, never mind the fact that when I kissed her my entire body responded with a resounding *No más!*

We made our way back to my dorm room, and pretty immediately this girl, whose name I can't remember so let's just call her Jessica because every girl born in the late '80s was a Jessica, said she wanted to have sex with me. I was having all this anxiety—I was not turned on, and I'd never done this with a girl. I'd never had penetrative sex with anyone! So I defaulted to the easiest excuse I could think of. The low-hanging fruit.

Welp! I don't have a condom! Better luck next time!

But no. This bitch threw on a pair of my boxer shorts and started storming down the hall knocking on as many doors as she could. She was DETERMINED to get a condom, and, give her credit, get a condom she did. Not five minutes later, Jessica came bounding into my room holding up that Trojan like she'd found Willy Wonka's golden ticket: "All right, let's do it!"

And look, I tried. A little. There was some light foreplay, but it became clear pretty quickly that my junk was not working. It was just not getting erect. And I started to panic a little, because I was scared that Jessica would tell my friends what happened, and that they would figure out I was gay. By this point, I had no confusion about my sexuality. I knew I was gay. In addition to my relationship with Nolan, I had hooked up with one other guy, and I was flirting with boys on MySpace. There was a strange art form to social media flirting back then. You could usually tell by looking at someone's profile if they might be gay, so when someone I didn't know would add me, I had a pretty good idea what it was about. Sometimes, I'd add cute guys for the same reason, and a very beating-around-the-bush no-paper-trail flirting process would ensue. The second boy I ever kissed was a guy I chatted with on MySpace who was coming to North Carolina for a cheerleading competition (clearly I had a type), and I went to meet him not explicitly thinking we were going to hook up but . . . you know how that story ends.

All of which is to say, the failed attempt with Jessica wasn't some major revelatory moment for me. But I was in the closet, so I was scrambling, trying to stall and keep things from escalating when suddenly, to my saving grace and rescue, Justin came back to the room and loudly flung the door open. I'm pretty sure he knew we were in there—he was trying to be funny and fuck with us a bit—but little did he know he straight-up saved the day.

After that, even I couldn't help but laugh at myself. *Okay, bitch, I see you. How are you going to continue with this farce if you can't even get it up to have sex with a girl?*

It's not like I came out the next day, but it became pretty clear after that evening that my days in the closet were numbered.

That summer, I moved to New York City for a summer internship. I'd had this fantasy that I could escape North Carolina for a bit and live my life as an out gay man, and that's what I did. I didn't pretend to like girls, or to be into anything I wasn't, and—surprise!—it was pretty goddamn freeing.

It was during that summer that I went to my first Pride, a rite of passage for any gay man—or any human being who enjoys happiness and fun. Broadway Dance Center, where I was interning and taking classes, was full of homosexuals like me, so I quickly made a lot of friends. One of those friends was the front desk manager, Anthony, who gave me his ID to use as my fake. He was five-eight to my six-two and looked absolutely nothing like me but whatever, it did the trick. I had plenty of foolish drunken nights thanks to that man, so Anthony, I appreciate you.

One of those nights was in June 2006. Anthony invited me to join him at a rooftop Pride party on Christopher Street, right across from the Stonewall Inn. Being there, oh my god it was such a vibe. Bare nipples and assless chaps as far as the eye could see, everyone celebrating themselves and their gender and their sexuality—it was magical. There is truly nothing like New York Pride. The city is the birthplace of the gay rights movement, and while Pride is special to me every year because it reminds me of family and community and the importance of loving ourselves, to spend my very first Pride watching the floats roll past the Stonewall, where it all began? I didn't appreciate the significance of it at the time—all the work that space represents or the hardship that went into getting society to accept queer people. I wasn't thinking about social justice or the gratitude I should have to the trans and queer trailblazers who came before me, those who put their lives at risk so I could party on that rooftop. I was thinking about how happy I was. How much lighter I felt. The weight had been lifted and I was watching gay people living positive and joyful lives and I finally made up my mind that I wanted that for myself.

And so, my coming-out journey began. First, I told Kacie. I broke the news over AOL Instant Messenger (it was college; AIM was still a thing back then), and because she was one of the first people I came out to, and I guess I wasn't ready to fully take the leap, I told her I was bisexual. Not to delegitimize bisexuality, but a lot of gays land there before they come out, and I was not someone who was actually bi. She was very accepting of my fake bisexuality, and then was very accepting *again* when I came out completely.

I told Justin, my longtime best friend and college roommate, in a MySpace message. Clearly I was scared and not ready for face-to-face conversations, and I think I wanted a buffer so he could have a minute to process. Even the phone seemed too intense, too direct. This was someone who I'd been hiding a lot of myself from for years, and I knew it might come as a shock. It took him a couple of days to respond, but eventually Justin wrote me back with kindness and care and acceptance, and our friendship remained intact.

Eventually there was only one person left to tell: my mom. I had anxiety about it, not because I thought she'd disown me or behave in any horrible way, but because I feared being a disappointment and I was nervous about how the discussion would go.

Still, if I wanted to fully embrace my new freedom, this was the last box to check. I lived at home my sophomore year of college, and every day I would think, *Today will be the day,* but then she'd come home late or I'd be tired or she'd have a bad day or I'd be heading out the door. The timing was never right, but the anxious energy around it was building up in me like a pressure cooker threatening to explode.

One day my mom came home from work to find me sitting in the kitchen, clearly on edge. I wasn't planning for this to be the day, but I was also feeling mad at myself for continually kicking the can down the road. I was scared to take the plunge and sad that I was still in hiding. I guess she could tell something was weighing on me.

"What's wrong?" she said as she puttered around the kitchen, getting herself dinner.

That simple question was enough to get my tears flowing.

"Why are you crying?" she asked.

"Mom, I have to tell you something," I said.

She looked straight at me, ready to hear whatever I was about to say.

"I'm gay."

Now she was crying, too. For me, the tears were an emotional release more than anything. I'd been holding something inside for years, and to finally let it out to the most important person in my life was a huge relief. As for my mom, I imagine her tears were for a combination of reasons. Her first response, which is pretty common among parents of gay men, was that she just wanted me to be safe. She was scared about HIV. I imagine she also felt a little bit of grief for the life she had always imagined for me, or for herself. But overall, my mom was loving and accepting. The conversation went as well as I could have hoped.

There is no way to articulate how free I felt after that.

With this giant secret no longer weighing me down, I could stop holding back the tendencies that I'd subconsciously worried were "too gay" or "too girly." My fashion, especially, could finally go to the next level. A big part of how I expressed myself back then (and now too) was in the way I dressed. Some of my fashion choices back then are cringe as fuck now—so much time in UGGs!—but I was all about loud prints and colors and basically anything that screamed THIS GUY IS GAY. I started listening to the music that by high school I had decided wasn't masculine enough, like Britney and Janet Jackson and Robyn. (In middle school I'd been innocent enough to listen to Britney with no shame, but as I got older I knew I would be judged for being "too gay" so I took a break.) I didn't have to live in fear of my secret getting out, or of being judged by the people who loved me, so I let go and became more of my full-out (no marking), extra, wonderful self.

Coming out is messy and complicated and it can be beautiful and it can be really dark. But it absolutely forces queer people to look at qualities about ourselves that we might feel shame or guilt or discomfort about and really process those emotions, come to terms with them, and ultimately love ourselves in spite of them. Coming out forced me to embrace the things about myself that I once hated, or at least hid—the fashion and the music and my love of dancing. The plight of being in the closet is that you are constantly analyzing your mannerisms, your actions, your words, your likes, and your dislikes. You're always wondering if one of those things is going to out you or earn you ridicule. You might express that you like a certain outfit, or say something with a certain intonation, and if it causes anyone to raise an eyebrow you're forced to explain it away or justify it. It's a constant self-analysis just to protect yourself, and I was over it.

Staying true to who I was became the guiding principle of my life, and the effort that went into that introspection was important work. It's something that nonqueer people simply don't have to do at an early age—or maybe at any age—because they're already accepted for who they are. Because the thing is—gay, straight, bi, whatever—we all have things we may not like about ourselves. Qualities that are maybe outside the norm and that we wish were different. Now imagine you could let go of the shame associated with those things and instead show yourself grace and compassion. Imagine we all took a minute to ask ourselves the hard questions: *What brings me joy? What are my values? What kind of people do I want to surround myself with?* I think the fact that we've been forced to grapple with these questions is why there's so much love in the LGBTQ community. We've had to make choices about the kind of energy we want in our lives. We've had to be deliberate about who we let in, and, in some cases, who we don't.

There's a lot of debate these days about whether gay people should even have to come out. The argument against the official "coming out" moment is that a person's sexuality isn't reliant on other people knowing, or that it's only one part of our identity, or that we should be able to keep things private from certain people if we want. Straight people don't have to come out as straight, so why do we need to announce that we're gay? I get it. But I still believe that coming out is important, because it takes a lot of courage.

The act of coming out, every time it's performed, adds visibility to gay issues and the gay experience. And for people who are still scared or unsure, it's helpful to see the freedom and happiness and lightness that coming out can afford. Because, listen, I am so happy that I'm gay. Even if I *could* choose a different life, I wouldn't. Being gay is fun! There's a reason why having a gay best friend—or wishing you had one—is a middle-aged lady's beloved cliché, and it's not because we're a token or a trophy. It's because we've learned how to accept and love a part of ourselves that we once hated, and who doesn't want to be around that kind of radical self love?

A MEDITATION FOR SELF-LOVE, FROM ME AND MAMA RU

When I was training to be a certified meditation instructor, I went on a retreat where I learned a meditation that has always stuck with me. It's constantly floating in the back of my mind, reminding me to have compassion for myself. Perhaps it can do the same for you.

Visualize your younger self. Don't just think about *being* younger; really imagine the person you once were, standing in front of you, as if that kid is an entirely separate person from the person you are now. Notice the missing teeth or the baby face or the blond hair or grass-stained knees of your innocent childhood self.

Now think about what that kid is dealing with. What they might be worrying about or curious about or confused about. Think about what they are equipped to handle and understand. Maybe this makes you feel protective, or sympathetic. Maybe it makes you want to embrace that little kid and tell them that all the best is yet to come. Maybe you want to say, "You're great just the way you are," or "Don't lose that sense of joy!" or "You *will* find your people one day."

There's something about observing your former self through your adult lens that allows you to be more understanding and kind to the childhood you. You give that former self love and compassion, and it helps you give that same love and compassion to your current self.

In my own meditation, I picture the little boy with the blond hair and the neon-pink Mickey Mouse shirt and I think about what he was dealing with—not having a father, having an addict for a mother, being a latchkey kid, feeling all these confusing sexual thoughts and fears about having a safe home and enough money for food—and I wish I had a time machine. I wish I could talk to myself (it's against the rules of time travel, I know) and tell that kid that everything will be all right and that he's good enough and he will make it through. It's like the finale of *RuPaul's Drag Race,* when Ru shows the finalist a photo of their younger self and every queen starts to cry because they want to protect that inner child. It's a deep release, because so much of our trauma and the shit we're in our heads about stems from our childhood. If Mama Ru were standing in front of me with a photo of Little Cody, I'd say, *You'll be okay. It'll take work to understand this, but some of the side effects of those hardships—the work ethic, the ability to entertain a crowd—they're the very traits that will allow you to thrive.*

That would be followed by a one-minute speech about my track record and why I deserve to be America's next drag superstar . . . wait, am I getting too deep into this fantasy?

CHAPTER THREE

Big-City Energy

The summer before my freshman year of college, Kacie suggested we take a road trip to New York City. At that point, New York wasn't on my radar. I was not one of those small-town gays obsessing over *Sex and the City* and dying to drink cosmos with Carrie and Samantha at a bar in the Meatpacking District. I never really watched *Sex and the City* until my boyfriend and I binged it about five years ago, when we first started dating. But back in the late '90s or early 2000s, when the rest of America was debating Big vs. Aidan? Not me. You think Cindy Rigsby could afford HBO? No, ma'am.

But I didn't need to idealize Manhattan to know that it was probably better than Greensboro. When Kacie suggested a road trip, I was just happy to have an opportunity to get outta Dodge. We took our adult-wannabe selves to the nearest Borders bookstore, ordered chai lattes, and dug up the Lonely Planet and Not for Tourists and Frommer's guidebooks and started to craft our big-city itinerary. A few weeks later, we booked a hotel on the Upper West Side, packed up my Kia Sephia, which was already holding on for dear life, and thought, *Yes, great idea, let's take this baby for an eight-hour drive up north!*

Somehow we made it in one piece, and I know it sounds cheesy to say it was love at first sight, but when I arrived in New York . . . it was love at first sight. We did all the touristy stuff—the Toys"R"Us in Times Square (RIP), Central Park, the American Museum of Natural History, the Museum of Sex (we were eighteen and goddammit we were gonna do something cah-razy), and tons of Ray's Pizza because Kacie, to this day, still eats pepperoni pizza once a week. We stopped short of the Statue of Liberty, but otherwise we really leaned into the tourist motif. And we were so excited to go shopping in Manhattan together. Remember, this was the friend with whom I would drive ninety minutes to Urban Outfitters, the one with whom I shared the "Style of Their Own" title in the high school yearbook. Our first day in New York we went straight to H&M and we thought we were The Shit.

There was something about the energy of New York that I found completely captivating. There was constant movement, a go-go-go vibe that matched my hustle even back then. Kacie was into it, too, but perhaps because she had a less urgent desire to escape Greensboro than I did, she wasn't like, *Imma move here but quick.* I, on the other hand, was very much like that.

That road trip planted a seed for me, and by the time we were heading back down south I'd hatched a plan: I would return to Greensboro for my freshman year of college, take that time to apply to schools in New York, and transfer to the Big Apple to start my sophomore year. And I went through with it . . . to a point. I applied to Marymount Manhattan College and AMDA—the American Musical and Dramatic Academy—because I was still trying to be an actor. And I got into both of them. But then I took a good look at the tuition fees and realized, because I'm no fool, that I was not going to go hundreds of thousands of dollars in debt to get a degree. Especially one from AMDA, which is not even a degree but a fucking certificate. Nope. Uh-uh. There's a reason they call that place SCAMDA.

It's a good thing I knew better, too, because it didn't take long into my college career for me to realize that musical theater was not my destiny. It was my major during freshman year, but I didn't book any roles in any of the shows, because the truth of the matter is that I can't sing. This girl was meant for the dance floor. In middle school, I watched MTV every day after school, teaching myself the moves from the day's top videos. My mom would pick me up from school and we would go to the Greensboro Coliseum so she could finish her catering shift, and while she was setting up the dining room I would watch *TRL* on the TV above the bar and take breaks during the commercials to do my homework. And this was back before YouTube and DVR. You couldn't pause or rewind. I had two minutes to watch a pop star shake their ass on TV and pick up whatever moves I could, and I did. I could move my body and catch a beat, and when I had the chance—at the middle school dances, or my mom's work holiday parties—I could draw a crowd.

During my freshman year of college, right around the time I realized I was not an actor, my friend George told me about an internship he'd done at Broadway Dance Center, the legendary studio in New York. It sounded like a great opportunity and also a ticket into the New York City dance world. Interns essentially took eight to ten dance classes a week for all of June and July, while also doing a work-study at the studio, and then paying tuition on top of that. I love how they called it an internship and then charged students $3,000 to enroll. What a racket.

I showed up in New York City that summer with *maybe* $1,600 in my bank account and an American Express card that I was irresponsible with. (Deadass, I did not pay off that AmEx until I got my first bonus at Peloton ten years later.) I'd found a room in an apartment on some wannabe-craigslist that wasn't actually craigslist (for anyone who's ever found an apartment, roommate, or couch on craigslist, you understand how sketchy this was—it was like going-to-a-Grindr-hookup-without-seeing-their-face kind of scary . . . girl, is the dick worth it?), so I had no idea if it was legit, but I crossed my fingers. I'll never forget touching down at Newark airport, with my giant suitcase and over-size canvas army bag that didn't have wheels. I was a sweaty, hot disheveled mess, far from the aspiring ingenue they show arriving to the Big Apple in the movies. With all my cumbersome shit it would have been best to jump in a cab, but to quote Kristen Wiig in *Bridesmaids*, "Help me, I'm poor." I had to take the train. I lugged my massive suitcase from Newark to Penn Station, and then from Penn Station to Washington Heights, which, if you don't know Manhattan, is a hike. And it was hot. So fucking hot. Like BLAZING. And, oh my god, I got on the subway with my massive suitcase and giant bag, and I was just, like, petrified. Not because I was scared of the subway or didn't know my way around New York, but because I was the girl with two massive bags taking up a huge amount of space on public transit—a New Yorker's worst nightmare.

Eventually, I made it to my apartment. Excuse me, my room in someone else's apartment. That room had no air conditioner, no door, and I lived with a sixty-year-old *abuelita* who was also a nurse. Lord knows I got on her nerves that summer. I was not the best roommate, and she would always read me for leaving a mess and not doing the dishes—all reasonable, but at that age I *was* a mess. Somehow, she put up with me for two months. Even after she found a dead mouse in the floor fan in my room.

Soon after I arrived, my internship began. I was supposed to man the front desk a few times a week as a part of my work-study, but luckily Broadway Dance Center also had a pre-professional program, and I learned that I could complete all my work-study hours for the entire summer in one week if I joined the production crew for that program's dance showcase. I immediately signed up.

On the first day of the gig, I was standing backstage in the sound booth with another freelance theater tech who was working the showcase with me. She was a biracial girl with short curly hair and big Coke-bottle glasses—a real cool-nerd vibe—and she was so sweet. I opened up to her immediately.

"Thank God we got this job," I said. "I can't be doing work-study every week for eight weeks, I need to get a real job, one that pays. I have literally $1,600 in the bank, which I need to cover rent and food and my social life. How long will that last me in New York? A week? Two? I gotta figure it all the fuck out."

"I'm actually quitting my job soon," she told me. "I work on the Upper West Side at this lampshade store. It's pretty boring—you're selling custom lampshades to rich people—but my boss is nice and the pay is decent and I feel bad that I'm ditching him, so I'd love to help find my replacement. Want me to recommend you?"

God bless this girl. "Yes! Please!" I said. "Let there be light!"

By my second week in New York, I had finished my entire summer's worth of work-study. Coke-Bottle-Glasses (I wish I could remember her name, truly) followed through with her offer and scored me a job interview at her fancy-ass custom lampshade store, Oriental Lamp Shade, on Seventy-ninth between Broadway and Amsterdam. I showed up for my interview expecting some snobby old woman to be running the show. Instead, the manager of the store walked out from the back office, and, praise God, he was an older gay who took one look at me and was immediately obsessed. Not, like, obsessed in a sexual way; he was just obsessed with my vibe. He hired me on the spot. It really warms my heart to think about it now. Here was an elder gay looking out for a younger gay, and, ugh, I appreciate that. (Although, I must admit, I lied and said I was in New York for good, which I knew was not the case. The beginnings of a shady career . . . literally and figuratively.)

So that was my first summer in New York. I worked full-time at the lampshade store, making twelve bucks an hour. It was a miserable job, but I got to see the wealth in New York City firsthand, because only rich-ass people who live uptown are buying multiple custom lamp shades for their apartments or (and!) their Hamptons homes. Every day I was simultaneously incredibly bored and incredibly awed at how rude people with money can be. But I was fortunate—I had a stream of income coming in, I could still make my dance classes, and I somehow had a thriving social life.

Wow. To be nineteen. So much energy. I'm exhausted just thinking about it. The work, the classes, the partying.

Still, I cannot stress enough how much I loved that summer in New York. Loved. I was hustling and bustling, but it didn't break me down. If anything, it fueled me. There are people who would have never returned to New York after that summer. Those eight weeks would have scratched the itch and sent them on their way. But not me. I loved the energy of the city and craved more of it. I've always been someone who wants to stay busy and in motion—I'm uncomfortable being idle, which is something I've been working on in my adult life—so yes, it was hard keeping all those balls in the air, but I knew that there was opportunity in this city. I didn't know exactly what I wanted to do or who I wanted to be, but I knew that those truths were waiting to be discovered in New York. The city was dripping with possibility.

CHAPTER FOUR

Cindy

There's no person on this earth who has had as much influence on me as my mom. I know that's true for lots of people, but if you know me—in person, or from my rides—you know Cindy.

My mom had me when she was thirty-three, and she was happy to have waited until then. She's told me since I was young that I shouldn't settle down until my thirties, and, like most of the advice she's shared over the years, that stuck with me. When I reached my twenties and people around me started getting married or having kids, I thought they'd lost their minds. (I should note, kids really aren't for me. I like my money and my vacation time. By the time I'm old, the robots will take care of me.) It's a testament to the fact that no matter how complicated our relationship has gotten—and over the years it's gotten pretty fucking complicated—hers is the wisdom I take to heart. I am nothing if not Cindy's son.

Growing up, my mom wasn't a regular mom, she was a cool mom . . . and if you missed that *Mean Girls* reference, yes, I'm judging you. So many of my favorite memories from childhood revolve around silly moments with Cindy.

Like one afternoon, after it had rained a lot in California (a rare occurrence), she put me in the car, rolled down the windows, and drove really fast through the streets of our neighborhood to let the water splash in like an amusement park log-flume ride. I was probably seven, and I thought it was the best day ever. When I got older, there would be days, maybe once a quarter, where I would wake up in a bad mood or complaining about school and she'd just say, "Do you want to play hooky? If you don't want to go to school today, you don't have to. We could go to the movies and have a day together." We didn't do this all the time, but it was enough to make an impression. My mom doesn't always play by the rules or take life too seriously, and I've always appreciated that about her.

If I inherited some of my silliness and my levity from my mother, the same is true of my bitchiness. One afternoon when we still lived in California, we were going to the Glendale Galleria for a little shopping trip. Finding parking in L.A. is atrocious, and my mom was about to pull up on a parking space when some lady cut her off and took the spot. "What a cunt!" my mom yelled. It was the first time I'd ever heard the word. *I don't know what that word is,* I thought, *but, fuck, I know it's not nice! Never heard those four letters, but woooooo I know they are not okay!* Cindy is a woman who will say what's on her mind with absolutely no filter. We'll be walking down a New York City street and she'll spot a lady ten feet in front of us and blurt out "Oh, that girl's dress is . . . interesting" without giving it a second thought. Recently, I was preparing to go to Matt Wilpers's wedding and I wanted to wear a skirt. When I could barely fit into the one I'd chosen she just looked at me and said,

"Well, I guess you won't be having any cake." She also told me that when she was younger she had a threesome, and all I could think was, *Of course you would tell me this.* At a recent birthday dinner in SoHo, there was a group of mostly bald fortysomething white guys at a table next to us. She took one look and turned to me and said, "They all seem to look alike, don't they?" I nearly spit out my drink. She was my first partner in gossip, and has a way of pointing out the obvious that always has you second-guessing whether or not she's being shady.

By the time I got to high school, Cindy's "cool mom" status manifested in different ways. I was a kid who liked to party—not irresponsibly, but certainly as much as any red-blooded American teenager. One day I was in the shower and my mom went to grab something out of my car, where I had beer in the trunk (back in those days, my McDonald's coworkers would buy me booze). She stuck her head in the bathroom door and held up a six-pack of Bud Light. "Do you want me to put this in the fridge?" she asked. She didn't really care if I had alcohol, but she would drop me off at parties or pick me up so that I wasn't driving drunk. It was always, *I know you're going to do this, so let's make sure it's being done responsibly.* She accepted the reality of what it meant to be a teenager, so instead of fighting with me she focused on keeping me safe.

I don't know exactly when my mom got clean, but I don't think she was using drugs once we moved to Greensboro. She did, however, go to a methadone clinic there. I didn't understand much about what that meant as a kid; it was just a truth of our lives. She also had mental health struggles—my mother is bipolar and suffers from anxiety—

which I couldn't wrap my head around back then. What I did understand, even though she tried to shield me from it, was that we were broke.

Our family's financial struggles were a constant cloud looming over our lives. It wasn't just that I couldn't afford name-brand shoes or that we lived in a small apartment. There were no birthday parties. There were Christmases without presents. Our money problems came to a head when I was in sixth grade. One afternoon I walked outside after school, and there was my mom in her boyfriend's massive pickup truck. She didn't usually pick me up, but on this day she drove up in a car that was filled to the brim with the contents of our home. It looked like *The Beverly Hillbillies*, a lifetime of shit packed into the bed of a pickup. It turned out my mom had botched the rent and we'd been evicted, so she dumped our furniture and clothing and all our stuff into the truck and grabbed me from school before heading to a storage unit and checking us in to a motel.

I'd known things were bad with our finances, but I was a middle schooler—I didn't know the severity of the situation until that day. Believe me, it doesn't matter how old you are, nothing says "The outlook is bleak" like staring down a truckload of your own belongings because you don't have a permanent home. In that moment, shit got very real.

We ended up moving into an extended-stay motel. My mom and her boyfriend slept in the bed and I slept on the floor, though I often spent weekends with my mom's friend Glenda, or stayed with classmates for weeks at a time. I was lucky to have friends with generous families who were willing to take in another preteen boy, but of course I found the entire situation embarrassing. No, it was more than that, if I'm being honest. Living in a motel when you are twelve is traumatizing. I tried to normalize it, since this was my life, but there is so much shame that accompanies an unstable living situation. Not to mention the fact that, to my twelve-year-old self, the circumstances were confusing. My mom was finally holding down a job, and my grandfather had recently passed away and left my mom an inheritance, which came in monthly checks. (My grandfather was no dummy, and he must have known that my mother didn't have the greatest sense of responsibility, so one lump sum wasn't happening.) On the surface, it was the most money we'd ever had, which made it hard for me to comprehend why we couldn't find a home. Now I understand that while we lived off the inheritance and the paychecks, my mom's credit was shit, which makes it hard to secure a permanent residence.

We lived in that motel for a little over a year. It was a shitty time, made not at all better by the presence of my mom's boyfriend, Donald. I didn't particularly like Donald. To be fair, he didn't do anything specific to make me not like him—he tried to be nice and friendly and establish a relationship, but I was not receptive to him or his friendship. First of all, until Donald came around during sixth grade, I'd never seen my mom with a boyfriend. Having a third person in our life felt foreign, and I didn't like having to share my mother with someone else. I was very much an only child. I also wasn't used to having another person in my home, or lack thereof. This was a motel—there was hardly room for two of us, and there definitely wasn't room for three of us. Sharing space with him was uncomfortable, so I was avoidant and, frankly, I had hard feelings.

And, of course, Donald came with his own baggage, literally and figuratively. Like my mother, he was an addict, and I'm pretty sure he and my mom met at the clinic. Over the years their relationship became toxic. They were completely codependent, for companionship but also out of necessity—Donald had a car and he helped with housing costs. My mom hadn't had someone for a long time, and she was lonely, and there was definitely a circumstantial element to the relationship.

After I spent about a year shuffling between the motel, friends' houses, and Glenda's house, my mom got us a place to live. The three of us moved into a house in Greensboro, where we stayed for four years. It was nice to be out of the motel, but life with a mentally ill addict is never exactly settled. Moments of chaos were part of the pattern long before we'd moved into the motel, and they would remain so long after we got out. Like one day in middle school, when my mom asked me to order a pizza. I called Domino's and asked for one medium pie. A treat! But then, when the delivery boy arrived with the food, my mom decided it was too expensive. "What the fuck is this?" she screamed. "Fifteen dollars for a medium pie? What, you think we're rich? Like I'm just going to buy you dinner because you want to order in?" She flipped her shit and eventually threw the entire pizza on the floor and stormed out of the room, leaving me utterly confused, just staring at the sad Domino's box on the floor.

Donald's presence was not helping our family dynamic.

My mom didn't seem happy with him, and I didn't want to live with him anymore, so eventually I asked her to move into a new apartment without him. The only way this would be possible, I knew, was if I helped pay the rent.

My mom didn't ask me to chip in, but I wasn't blind. It became a running theme of our relationship—the only way we'd get out of one bad situation or another was if I made it happen, and so I had to step up. I want to say I always did so happily, but by then I was a seventeen-year-old working multiple jobs to help support a fully grown adult. What seventeen-year-old is happy to help pay the rent? Still, I knew I had to ensure my mom wasn't living in an unsafe situation, so I bit the bullet. I had money from my McDonald's job—a job I got because I wanted my own cash and my own freedom and independence. I swore I would never again be without a place to stay or forced to scrounge through the couch for food money. I took a job to take care of myself, not so that I could be my mom's provider or protector. It hadn't even occurred to me that it would come to that. And, I should point out, keeping that job wasn't easy. Before I saved up enough for a car, the only way I could get to work was to ride the public bus for an hour—the McDonald's was only fifteen minutes away, but the bus had a lot of stops so of course it quadrupled the time. I had to run out of class at the end of the day to make it to the bus stop across the street in front of the community college. Riding public transportation in a big city is run of the mill; doing so as a teenager in Greensboro was embarrassing. By the time I saved up enough to buy myself a car and pitch in for the rent, I'd been working my ass off. So you can imagine my frustration when I had to lend my mother my car every day so that she could get to work. All my classmates were driving to school, and I was getting dropped off and picked up by my mommy. When you're in high school, you just want to live like the other kids. You want your mom to take care of *you*, not the other way around.

And this, I have learned from many hours of therapy, is where my resentment began. Ultimately my frustrations were simple: Why wasn't my mother working as hard as I was to help us make ends meet? Why wasn't she doing more to keep us afloat, and why did that fall to me? Couldn't she put in a little more effort? I was the child and she was the parent, but it felt like I was putting in the sweat while she was taking it easy. I never considered *not* providing for my mom, or *not* working as hard as I did, but I was frustrated—and, I know now, angry—that it all seemed to be my burden.

When I left for college to live in the dorms, my mom could no longer afford the apartment that we had been sharing, so she once again moved in with Donald. Eventually, he relapsed into alcoholism, which we realized when we noticed a bottle of tequila in the fridge had gone down significantly, quickly. My mother came home one day, after dating Donald on and off for nearly a decade, to find him attempting suicide in the bathtub. That was the end of their relationship, so I left the dorms and moved back in with her so that we could afford a place together. By that point we were splitting the rent fifty-fifty, and it was certainly a bit embarrassing to be living with my mom as a college student. But the bottom line was always the same: If I didn't help her, she wouldn't help herself. I saw the truth in front of me, and so I handled it.

I have done a lot of work over the past decade to unpack and process my feelings around my childhood circumstances, but I couldn't have clearly stated how I was feeling back then other than to say I was getting annoyed and fed up. When I graduated college, all I knew was that I wanted to move to New York. I graduated in 2009—the country was in a recession, and while my mom had been working as a waitress until that point, she, like so many others, lost her job. In fact, to this day, that was the last time my mom was consistently employed. I, on the other hand, had been offered a job in New York at Wild Child Nation, a streetwear brand founded by Luam, a choreographer who I'd taken classes with at Broadway Dance Center and later worked with on *Dancing with the Stars*. It was the first time in my life that I decided to choose myself over my mom. I didn't have the means to fully support her, and I didn't want to give up on my own aspirations. I had to be selfish. I wasn't trying to hang my mother out to dry, but I had to deliver a hard message: *I've done a lot to provide for you and make sure you're taken care of, and I can't help anymore. I cannot put all my dreams aside because you can't get your shit together.* It may have been harsh, but I was exhausted by the pattern of instability and the "Cody will take care of us" narrative. That story, which I know I helped craft, had taken a toll on our relationship. It was time to take care of myself.

ONCE YOU POP,
YOU CAN'T STOP

Snacks I ate in the '90s that still hit . . . and some that really, really miss.

HIT: Cool Ranch Doritos
A wet hand in a Cool Ranch Doritos bag . . . is there anything more summer? Your six-year-old self just got out of the pool, you've got pruney wet hands, your mom told you not to put your grimy fingers in that damn bag but sorry, girl. Summer.

MISS: Hot Pockets
Who is still eating a Hot Pocket? That nuclear jacket it wears? What is that?! How is it possible that these radioactive paninis have ice crystals, and yet one bite into them burns the roof of your mouth?

HIT: Cheez-Its
By far the superior baked-cheese snack. Get out of my face with a Cheese Nip—what even is that? Same with Goldfish. Those are for children. If it ain't a Cheez-It, I don't want to sees it.

MISS: Choco Taco

Like a relationship where you said *I love you* only 'cause you didn't know what else to say back, you won't miss what you didn't have. Farewell, Choco Taco, I've finally found real love.

HIT: Cheesy Gordita Crunch

Pro tip: Now they make a Doritos version. One thing about Taco Bell, they are going to get creative with these menu items. I don't hate it.

MISS: Pizza Hut Buffet

In the '90s, you couldn't get a better pizza than Pizza Hut buffet pizza. Those crispy edges? And that salad bar? Iconic! The quality is trash now. Once a fine institution that promoted childhood literacy through the BOOK IT! Program, now it couldn't even spell "quality ingredients."

HIT: Shirley Temple

Nothing made me feel more rich at the age of six than ordering a Shirley Temple. And there better be a cherry in there. Not only did it make me feel luxurious, it made me a little bitchy. Get one for your kids if you want to start them on their career path to Real Housewife.

MISS: Olive Garden

Y'all couldn't pay me to go to an Olive Garden today. For what? Some microwaved alfredo sauce and stale breadsticks? I live in New York City. Ain't no damn way. Eating at this establishment would force me to give up my status as a real New Yorker, something I worked ten years to achieve.

HIT: Halloween Oreos

I don't care what anyone says, that orange cream filling slaps. It tastes better than any other Oreo ever made. I don't know why, I don't work for the Oreo company, but it's true.

MISS: Black Licorice

Only people born before the Great Depression enjoy this snack. They say your taste buds change every seven years—I think we can safely say our society has collectively outgrown this one.

HIT: Dairy Queen Blizzard

But every time they turn it upside down, I do have a slight panic attack.

MISS: McDonald's Ice Cream

It tastes great, but is that machine ever working? I went by the drive-thru the other day and they had a sign hanging on the window: "No ice cream. No shakes." And I said, "No shit!" We already knew that! You didn't even have to put the sign up, McDonald's. We knew the machine was broken before we even got in line.

CHAPTER FIVE

Bag Lady

On July 7, 2009, I officially moved to New York. I'd love to tell you that life was all parties and good times and upward mobility after that but no, ma'am, that's not my legacy. That is not surviving in New York City. That would be boring.

No, I lived on one of the Wild Child Nation founders' couches for a month before I moved into another room on 167th and Broadway that I found on craigslist. It was another un-air-conditioned room in a walk-up in the heat of the summer. Has my entire life in New York been a sweat-drenched mess? Apparently. I had no TV in that room, I had the jankiest on-the-brink-of-dying computer that I bought for $300, and I had two roommates, one of whom was a Jamaican guy who would call his family every single night and scream into the phone as I was going to sleep. He and I shared a wall, and it was as if he were yelling to a group of people standing twenty feet away rather than talking on the phone. He shouted so loud in Jamaican patois, the Creole language he spoke with his family, and it kept me up every single night. It was haunting, but what the fuck could I do? I stuck that out for a bit until a friend of mine from my BDC internship told me there was an opening in her apart-

ment, which was about ten blocks away. It was four roommates and me, and I slept on a twin mattress on the floor
and paid $400 a month in rent. We had to put the rent, in
cash, in a box in the living room, and the landlord would
come by on the first of each month and take the cash out of
the box. I mean, *What?* (Eventually something happened
with our landlord. I honestly can't remember what, but she
started sleeping on our couch. She just moved right on into
the living room. I took that as my cue to move out. CHAOS.)

As you can probably tell, I was pinching pennies in those
days. I made maybe $35,000 working sales and production
at Wild Child Nation, and I would get off that job at night
and go to SoHo to work retail at Ben Sherman, the British
mod clothing brand. On weekends, I was working in Times
Square waiting tables at TGI Fridays. (Ugh, that disgusting
Jack Daniel's sauce. Why are you putting it on everything?
Just stop. It's drunk teriyaki sauce. Stop.) So yes, for those
doing the math at home, I absolutely did work three jobs at
once during my first six months in New York. And yes, I
still found time to go out and have a social life and take
more dance classes. I made a bunch of friends at the Ben
Sherman job, so we would usually go out on the Lower East
Side together on Friday nights after our shift. We'd get off
work at nine or ten and head to the Cock, a gay bar on Second Avenue, where I would drink whatever was cheap
enough to get me drunk quickly. I especially hit it off with
this one guy, Tommy, because shortly after we started working together we discovered we'd briefly dated the same guy,
and we trauma-bonded over that.

Tommy and I hung out a lot. One night, we tried to
sneak our way into a Fashion Week party. We were standing

outside, waiting at the door while another guy we knew, who was working the event, bartered with the doorman. Eventually, we got the go-ahead. I walked in, thinking I had Tommy's hand, and I don't know if I lost it or I never had it or what, but suddenly I was through the door and Tommy wasn't. There was nothing I could do. The door was shut behind me—I was inside, Tommy wasn't. I tried my hardest to get us both in, but I wasn't about to give up my night of glamour because my friend didn't move quickly enough. Sorry, babe, I'm gonna enjoy this! I'm not ruining my night because we didn't both get through the iron gates. I was all, "Take one for the team and I'll see you next time, bitch!" But Tommy was *pissed*. That was pretty much the end of that friendship.

Every night was some sort of similar adventure. I didn't sleep much, but when you first move to New York and you're young, you're barely in your apartment. You're always on the go—whether you're going to clubs or going to work—and I hated being home since my apartment was such shit, with my twin mattress and no TV, so what would I do there anyway?

Things took a turn in January 2010. Whether it was a turn for the better or the worse depends on your perspective. I'd been in New York for six months, and I was fucking exhausted, so I quit my TGI Fridays job and cut down my hours significantly at Ben Sherman. And then, because of course this would all happen at once, Wild Child was like, "Hey, girl, we can't afford you anymore, so we're going to have to lay you off." I went from having three jobs to having barely a part-time job in a matter of weeks. I had to go on unemployment and food stamps just to make it through. Thank God my rent was only $400 or my ass would have been headed back to Greensboro.

And yet! I think of that moment as a turning point more than a dark time, because I used it as an opportunity to really focus on my dance career. *I'm not working an office job, I don't have to juggle multiple shifts, maybe I should see where dance can take me.* I took on another work-study at Broadway Dance Center—it didn't pay but allowed me to take discounted classes—and immersed myself in dance. I was learning from big-time choreographers, surrounding myself with professionals, and starting to get initiated into the professional dance world. My first paid job was with Countess Luann—yes, the Real Housewife—for a perfor-mance of "Money Can't Buy You Class" at a Hamptons fundraiser. I was not a *Real Housewives* fan but at that point it was hard to be a person in the world, or at least a person who enjoys pop culture, and have no awareness of Countess Luann. The performance was anything but classy—Luann could hardly hold the vocal, so she certainly wasn't hitting the 5, 6, 7, 8. We really had to put in the work, which in-volved carrying Luann on our shoulders and throwing fake dollar bills into the crowd. I don't even think there was a proper stage, we just performed from somebody's front porch. But Luann was perfectly nice—she was definitely more nervous than we were—and, fuck, I made $600 and could finally say I was a working dancer.

Two important evolutions came out of that dance-focused phase: I started booking work regularly, and I met my friend Quintin. Both things seriously contributed to New York City finally feeling like home. First of all, being a dancer in New York was exciting! I was exposed to interesting and creative people, and I got to witness interesting and creative happenings, like the aforementioned New York Fashion Week and music video productions. But pursuing a dance career meant I had to consider returning to California and giving Hollywood a try. Los Angeles was where the big dance jobs were and where the casting was happening.

I took multiple trips—two weeks here, a month there— to see if I could audition and make L.A. work. But despite my California roots, the West Coast didn't feel right. First of all, the pace was so slow. To this day, one of my favorite things about New York is that the minute you step outside there's this energy that grabs you and pulls you along. It has a sense of urgency that L.A. just can't match. Plus, in New York, even if you're alone, you're constantly surrounded by people. In the subway, on the street, at the gym—even if you aren't actually *with* anyone else or talking to anyone else, it doesn't feel lonely. In L.A., I felt really alone. It's a car culture, which means you're driving by yourself a lot, and it was so isolating. And then when I did meet people, L.A. relationships felt incredibly transactional. Especially in the dance scene, every interaction had an undercurrent of What can you do for me?, which made me feel gross. I needed to get back to New York, where I felt comfortable, which reinforced the notion that I'd evolved from a transplant to a true New Yorker.

As for Quintin, I met him in Sheryl Murakami's jazz funk class at Broadway Dance Center. You may not recognize Sheryl's name, but believe me when I say you know her moves. She choreographed Beyoncé's "Run the World (Girls)" music video, for which she won an MTV Video

Music Award, as well as the "Ego" and "Dance for You" videos. Sheryl contributed to my success as a dancer, but she also taught me about being brash and upfront in my public persona. During the class in question, we were doing a dance to Ke$ha's "TiK ToK," and Sheryl had choreographed these little vignettes where dancers were in various stages of a hangover the morning after a big party. (It was a true shadowing of our soon-to-be-party-girl relationship.) At the beginning of the number she had me literally lying on top of Quintin like a drunk delinquent—that was how the dance kicked off—and it was the first time the two of us talked during class. That became an incredibly important friendship in my life—it still is incredibly important—and Quintin became something of my New York City sherpa.

First of all, he introduced me to the nightlife that would basically become a part of me. Don't get me wrong, I went out plenty before I knew Quintin, but the two of us, we really had a time. We were in our twenties, going out dancing four or five nights a week, brown-bagging Four Lokos before we went to the club. I want to vomit just thinking about it.

But there was another important element to my friendship with Quintin. He lived in Crown Heights, Brooklyn, with a bunch of his friends from Florida, which is where he grew up. It was an amazing roommate situation, especially compared to mine, which was pretty much one disaster after another. (I haven't even mentioned the apartment on the Upper East Side where I lived for a couple of months with a crazy old lady. One day I came home and there were EIGHT puppies in the living room, all of whom she had decided to foster on a whim. Don't ask me how I get myself into these predicaments. I do not know.)

I would trek to Crown Heights for group dinners with Quintin's roommates, and they became my chosen New York family. I started spending Thanksgivings there, because Quintin and my future roommate French would host Friendsgiving and it felt like this loving, comfortable, communal holiday gathering. A lot of young twenty-somethings in New York are like lost boys. We don't necessarily have traditional holiday celebrations to go home to, so we find one another and create our own traditions. My mom and I were close, and we talked on the phone all the time, but she was still in North Carolina and I was in New York, and neither of us had the means to visit the other. And the truth is, my mom had never cooked a proper Thanksgiving. We usually went to her friend Glenda's house, and when we didn't my mom would try to cook and it would be a total mess. So being in New York with my new friends allowed me to take ownership of the holiday and do it the way I wanted—we could drink a ton of wine and not worry about judgmental family members. It was one more thing that made the constant hustle worth it, because it gave me this sense of belonging that I really craved.

I always say that the people you meet when you first move somewhere probably won't be your friends for life, and it took until I met Quintin and his roommates (who eventually became my roommates, when a spot opened up in that apartment), for New York to truly feel like home and for me to feel like I had found my people. But there was literally *never* a moment where I considered throwing in the towel and giving up on New York. It's a badge of honor to be a New Yorker, because it's a hard city even in the best of times. As I always say, no matter how much money you have, no matter how successful you are, if you live in New York City, you will always be a bag lady.

But it wasn't like I stuck it out *despite* the hustle that was required to make it. I stuck it out *because* of the hustle. I look back now on the times when I was burnt out and broke and cold and on food stamps and, I don't know, I just loved it. I thrived in it.

CHAPTER SIX

Thank You for Being a Friend

Whenever I put a call out for "XOXO, Cody" questions, my DMs are flooded with requests for relationship advice. *How do I give feedback to a bad kisser? When is it time to dump his ass? What should I do if a guy can't get me off?* The questions are almost always about romance. People ask about dating and sex and breakups and marriage, but they almost never inquire about the relationships that I believe are the most important: friendships. Maybe that's because platonic relationships feel easier to master. I've seen people do some pretty shady shit to their friends, so I don't know that everyone has conquered the fine art of friendship as well as they might think. In fact, a little refresher might be in order, because this is one area (of many) where, yes, I have opinions.

First of all, let me just say, there's a reason why *The Golden Girls* is one of my favorite shows. I'm the classic mix of Dorothy in the streets and Blanche in the sheets. Those ladies knew what it meant to be a ride or die. They understood what so many of us often forget—that your friends will be in your life for much longer than the majority of your romantic relationships, so while you may get annoyed because Dorothy is being cranky or Rose is being spacey or Sophia is being the snarky queen that she is, you need to stick it out and show up for one another because you may be the last girls standing in your Miami bachelorette pad. And you're probably going to strike out a lot more with romantic partners than you are with friends, so you'll need your besties when things go south with a significant other, or when shit gets complicated and you need a shoulder to cry on.

Here's what I think people often forget—friendships take energy and intentionality. They should not be an afterthought. With romance, you've got oxytocin, that love drug, pumping through your veins. And that shit is strong! It will get you high as fuck. It's the reason you might laugh at bad jokes or get turned on by a man who plays the air guitar. But there's no friendship drug. With friends, you're building a relationship over good old-fashioned connection— whether it's an emotional bond, intellectual stimulation, or a common belief that JC Chasez was the true lead singer of NSYNC (I will die on that hill). And that means you can build a different and maybe even stronger foundation. Yes, there will be times when you're in the honeymoon phase of a romance, and you're acting a fool, ditching your friends for another night on the couch cuddling under a blanket watching *Love Is Blind.* We've all been there. But the hope is that you've invested enough energy into your friendships to earn those reclusive moments so that you won't be met with pushback or resentment when you're ready to rejoin the living and revisit your social life. Not just because you'll need those friends to lean on when you have relationship struggles, but also because you need them to weigh in when things *are* going well.

I don't have a ton of deal-breakers when it comes to romance, but if my friends don't approve of someone I'm dating, then I don't want him in my life. I don't understand people who are like, *I love him so my friends should love him.* I've always given side-eye to that *This is my partner, like 'em or leave 'em* approach. No. Good friends know you. They want the best for you. They observe your relationships from a different and more clearheaded vantage point, and they may be able to spot red flags or pressure points that are squarely in your blind spot. When my friends meet my partner, I'm asking them, *What do you think? Should I move forward? Do you see anything that I don't see?* And when my friends introduce me to their partners, they should be asking me the same things. These are simple rules of girl code.

I honestly do not think I would have survived life in New York thus far without my group of friends here. I call them my chosen family not to sound cute, but because they have supported me in every way possible—they've helped me through breakups, let me crash on their couches when I was in between apartments, and cheered me on as I found professional success. Quintin was the first member of this chosen family, but there was also my friend Oscar, who I met during a night out with friends and who became an important person in my life until he died of alcoholism in 2020. Also my friend David, who I have seen through med school and residency and who is now, like half the gays who go into medicine, an anesthesiologist. Then there's Patrick, my emotional teddy bear; Justin, a DJ and the guy I can talk politics with all day long; Andrew, one of the funniest people I know and a Broadway actor; and Cory, the friend who keeps all my secrets. These relationships, many of which started on the dance floors of New York City, have become crucial to my well-being. I feel incredibly fortunate to have found a group of gay men who are all ambitious and goal oriented and loving, but who also enjoy shaking their asses disrespectfully with me underneath a disco ball.

And while I call them my chosen family, even that moniker might be underselling it. There's an intimacy and honesty to close friendships that many of us don't necessarily have with, say, our parents. Friends are there on those messy nights, they see who you're hooking up with or how you behave when you're belligerently drunk, and they also see when you're successful at work or falling in love. They bear witness when you're discovering yourself, and that should not be underestimated. There's an intimacy to that kind of bond that is really fucking beautiful.

And that's why we have to love our friends, if not unconditionally, at least without judgment. Because part of being a true ride or die is letting your girlies do dumb shit or make mistakes without taking it personally. Not that I ever do dumb shit.

LOL. I jest. I can be a real messy bitch. Take, for example, my relationship with Michael, a guy I dated about a decade ago. Back then, I was spending a lot of time at big New York circuit parties. For the uninitiated, circuit parties are supercrowded gay parties at big venues or mega-clubs, where they play remixes of pop songs that basically sound like the song you know but with a lot of pots and pans banging in the background. Probably 90 percent of people are not sober at these affairs, and I'm not talking about alcohol—I won't be going into detail about what I put into my system back then, but let's just say it wasn't beer. One night, I started dancing with this guy, Michael, who wasn't especially good-looking and didn't have a banging body, but there was this charged energy between us that I couldn't get enough of. It didn't take long for us to start making out on the dance floor. I was completely mesmerized by him, and by the whole experience. He was a really good kisser, though it's possible my lack of sobriety had something to do with just how transfixed I was.

"Give me your number!" I yelled over the pots and pans.

"Okay!" he yelled back. "But I should tell you! I'm married!"

I learned that he had an Israeli husband who didn't have citizenship, so they were in a long-distance marriage. (This was before marriage equality.) Despite knowing better, I started hooking up with Michael regularly and eventually dating him . . . and, I thought, falling in love with him. All while he was married to someone else. Eventually he moved to Israel but we still kept talking on WhatsApp—then his husband found our messages and the whole thing was really fucking toxic. Go figure.

As all this was going down, my friends were definitely giving me side-eye. They knew I was crossing a line. But they didn't make me feel shitty about it, and when the relationship with Michael inevitably fell apart, they were my shoulders to cry on.

As long as your friends' behavior doesn't harm you, and

they aren't doing real harm to themselves, you've got to let the people in your life discover some truths on their own. And let's be clear—there's a difference between taking their dumb shit personally, which is something *you* have to fix, and letting their dumb shit cross a boundary that you've set to protect yourself. I absolutely advocate for self-preservation in relationships. If you're treating me poorly or in ways that are detrimental to my well-being, so long, sir. I will no longer be requiring your services. One star, do not recommend. But you have to give friends a little bit of grace and space to fail. Offer advice when asked, but unsolicited opinions . . . well, baby, think twice. I try to be the friend who chooses asking questions over giving advice, and a really important question is, "Do you actually want advice or do you just need me to listen?" Generally, your friends will be much happier if you allow them to come to conclusions about their lives on their own (even if you knew the right answers all along).

Not all my friendships have been runaway success stories. Shortly after I met Quintin, the two of us befriended a guy named Dylan, with whom I became very close. He lived in Hell's Kitchen and let me crash on his couch after especially messy nights when I didn't want to trek home to Washington Heights. Eventually, we decided to move in together in Astoria, Queens. It had all the makings of a great living situation, until things went real south, real fast.

First, we started fighting about chores and bills like an old married couple. "Why is the kitchen such a mess?" Dylan would ask. "Have you paid the electric bill? It's your turn to pick up cleaning supplies."

The nitpicking was constant, and it seemed to serve no purpose other than to get under my skin. It started to put a strain on our friendship, enough so that I started going out at night without him. This was a big change, because before we moved in together we were always doing things as a duo. This didn't go over well. I'd come home from a night out and get a passive-aggressive "How was *your* night? I was just at home," or sometimes more straightforward jealousy. There were often comments like "Oh, I guess he's your best friend now?" about whomever I was spending time with at the moment.

I'm not confrontational by nature, but this shit eventually got thoroughly uncomfortable. I had to say something. And so I told Dylan exactly what I was thinking: that he was in love with me. It was obvious! Why else would he be acting so fucking bizarre? Well, Dylan did not take kindly to my suggestion. He started throwing shit at me and breaking glasses on the ground like Glenn Close in *Fatal Attraction.* And then! This man took my clothes and started BURNING THEM. Yes, you read that right. He stood on our balcony setting my clothes on fire. He knew how to hit me where it hurt, too—he went straight for one of my favorite Mickey jackets and I watched it go up in flames. The whole episode told me that, first of all, YES, my hunch was right, he obviously was hung up on me, but also that, once again, it was time to find a new home.

The Dylan fiasco was an example of something I've come to accept over time—not all friendships last forever, and that's okay. I'm a loyal person. I've had a lot of abandonment in my life, whether it was my dad dying or my mom not being there or boyfriends leaving me, and I value loyalty above almost all else. For a long time, I subscribed to the idea that good people stay committed to a friendship no matter the ups and downs. But I've learned that there are instances when letting someone go is the healthiest option. Maybe the relationship is no longer serving either of you; maybe it's even hurting you. I've had multiple occasions where I've had to take breaks from friendships or create distance from someone who was important to me, and what I've realized over time is that those breaks have almost always been for the best. Sometimes they have even served the greater friendship, because we've been able to evolve separately and then come back together in a better place.

Not me and Dylan, though. No, ma'am. You burn my Mickey jacket, that's a wrap for me.

I had one friendship with a guy named Scott that was really tight for a while, almost brotherly. It may have been too brotherly, in fact, because over time the relationship energy evolved into something more competitive than familial. I'm not sure exactly what we were competing about—we weren't after the same men or the same job—but I always had this sense that he was trying to one-up me, or condescend to me, as if he were teaching me how to adult. One afternoon, we were hanging out at my place and I was making a sandwich. The refrigerator door was open, because I was pulling out the turkey, lettuce, bread, and mayo. "You really should shut that," he said. "You're wasting so much electricity."

Okay, Mom, chill out.

There was a constant undercurrent of tension in our relationship—we weren't frenemies, exactly, but sometimes we toed that line—and because we were both loyal people and loyal friends, we kept having these intense come-to-Jesus conversations and resets that eventually became more tiring than productive. It was a lot of "I don't appreciate it when you . . ." and "I know you mean well, but . . ." Not to mention, he would ask me for boyfriend and career advice, time and again, and then blatantly ignore it. That was his right, but when that disregard resulted in toxic relationships, I couldn't get on board. With one particular boyfriend, even after I warned Scott against it, he got engaged. I felt bad that I couldn't be happy for him, but I could not in good faith celebrate a relationship that I knew would have an ugly ending (and, make no mistake, the ending was busted). Plus, I just didn't get it. *Why do you keep coming to me for a shoulder to cry on and then repeat the same patterns? Why are you asking me for advice if you're never going to take it?* Eventually, I got to a place where I had to divest from the friendship. We did not have a big "breakup" moment, but we both started pulling away and stopped spending energy on each other so that we could stop repeating the same tired bullshit. These days, I still love Scott, but from afar. I've created a boundary. We are cordial when we see each other, but it's pretty surface level, and that has brought me a lot of peace.

All that said, here's my final word on friendship breakups: Be open to people coming back. I had a friend who I wanted to root for, but he was so hardheaded, so tough, and so resistant to feedback that it really seemed to be his way or the highway. He took a very *This is the way I am, accept it or don't* approach, and I started to close myself off to him as a result. But then he worked on his shit—he mended his relationship with his parents, he went to therapy, he started meditating. I could see this complete change in him. It was a great reminder that when you give people space and time and they actually use that space and time to do the work and better themselves, you can rekindle the relationship. It's hard to believe that people can change, especially if they've hurt you, but I've seen people I had great disdain for do complete 180s. And when that happens, your relationship usually becomes something stronger and more beautiful than you ever could have imagined.

Which brings me to a rule of friendship that even I still have to work on: Communicate! Tell your friends you're proud of them. Gas them up in the Instagram comments when they are slaying a photo. Cheer them on when they go on adventures, whether that's taking a new job, moving to a new city, or traveling around the world. And on the flip side, be honest with your friends when they've hurt you. The way we treat our friends sets the foundation for the way we treat ourselves, so if we aren't hyping them up when they succeed and forgiving them when they mess up, then it's going to be hard to do that for ourselves.

Honestly, I don't know why it's so difficult to say nice things out loud. I'll often have a nice thought about someone—that their ass is looking thick or their work is killer or they're particularly good at something—and move on with my day. But lately, I make a point to send a text or post a comment to articulate that thought. Be a true New Yorker—if you see something, say something! If we can't dish it out, we'll never be able to take it. And most of us need to learn how to accept love. (Related: Why is it so hard to accept a compliment? Just say thank you! Stop trying to diminish your accomplishments or explain away your success. No more, *It was nothing,* or *This old thing?* or *I don't know, I feel gross.* Enough! Own your victories, say thank you, move on.)

It's a universal truth that I wish was not the case: Showing love to others is easier than showing love to ourselves. Breaking down the barriers to self-love is a really hard thing to do, but it starts with expressing that love outward. If we hold ourselves back with our friends, we will absolutely do the same with ourselves.

So hang it on your wall, write it on your bathroom mirror, tattoo it on your arm if you must . . . The process of self-love starts with loving others. Say it with me.

One caveat, because I don't want any of you blaming Cody when things get weird: When I say you should show your friends love, I mean you should show it *emotionally.* One friendship complication I CANNOT support—and yes, you know what's coming . . . No! You cannot have sex with your friends! Once you cross that line, there's no going back. If a relationship starts as a sexual one and you end up being friends with that person, you've got to cut the sex. When you sleep with someone regularly, you don't want to get too attached, because you want the relationship to remain purely sexual. So, church and state. If you develop feelings for a friend and you start hooking up, then *that* becomes the relationship. You're not strictly banging, you're dating! There are feelings involved! And if you're just friends, you gotta stay friends. You cannot become friends with benefits and think that's going to work. When have you ever seen that work? Not for Justin Timberlake and Mila Kunis in *Friends with Benefits*! Not for Ashton Kutcher and Natalie Portman in that same movie with a different title! I don't understand sex with friends. It just doesn't make sense.

Friendships, like every good thing in life, are complicated. There are a million variables that can sneak in and wreak havoc. Sex and attraction, sure, but also jealousy and resentment. Because while the healthiest relationships are all about love and support, this is the real world. Healthy is the goal, but it's not always the reality. I know it can be hard to get excited for friends when they're hitting milestones or celebrating successes that you wish were yours. Here's what I say to that: Figure it out. Deal with the jealousy internally, and hype them up anyway. Learning to navigate feelings of envy or resentment is yet another way to practice self-love. Instead of fighting jealousy or letting it fester, recognize the feeling, acknowledge it, and let it pass. Learning to accept the negative emotions that come up about our friends' shit is the first step toward navigating negative emotions about our own shit.

And speaking of jealousy . . . if there is one way I know my own friendships are in a good place, it's that they've hardly changed a wink in the past five years. My life as a whole has changed dramatically—I've found professional success and financial security and a level of notoriety that I certainly didn't anticipate when I accepted a job at Peloton. But my friendships? No. The men in my life who were there for me when I was couch surfing after the clothes-burning chaos, or sitting across from me at those early Friendsgivings, are the same people who are cheering for me when I launch a new Peloton series or take on a new project. There are definitely moments when they're like, "Wow, girl, I can't believe what's happened to you," but they're proud of me and they celebrate my success, and it hasn't changed the way they approach me. They still call me out on my bullshit, thank God. These are, in many cases, decade-long friendships. We've given one another space to make mistakes and allowed each other to change and warmly welcomed those new-and-improved versions of ourselves. And because these are people who have stood by me since I was nothing, I want to do things for them now that I can. I want to pay for dinner or take them on trips, not as an act of charity but because these are my girls! I want to enjoy life with them. It's no fun to savor the spoils of success alone, so I want to share what I have with the people I love. Sharing is caring, people. It's a cliché for a reason.

XOXO, CODY:
READER QUESTION EDITION

Q: The guy I'm dating has a really big dick, but he's always in his feelings. It's too much! What should I do?

A: Sounds like you hit the jackpot. A well-endowed man who is also emotionally available?! What more could you ask for? Maybe you're the one who needs to work on vulnerability. My take? Let this man open your heart the way he's opening you up elsewhere.

Q: Is it cheating if you flirt with someone who isn't your partner? And if not, when does it cross the line? If you hook up? If you're emotionally intimate? If you keep it secret?

A: Flirting crosses the line when you or your partner disrespect the boundaries you've created in your relationship. It depends on what rules you've put in place. If yours is a monogamous relationship, flirting becomes cheating through physical contact—starting with kissing—or emotional intimacy. But I'd be more concerned about emotional intimacy than physical contact. The latter is a physiological need. Emotional intimacy is what you're looking for from a partner. If you're getting that from someone else, you're entering a danger zone.

Q: All my friends are in relationships except me. It's so discouraging. Any tips on staying positive about the single life when I really wish I had a partner?

A: Listen, sweetie. We're always going to think the grass is greener on the other side. When you're in a relationship, you want to be single. When you're single, you want to be in a relationship. Be happy where you are and enjoy the perks your situation offers. Trust timing, trust yourself, trust the universe. What's meant for you is gonna happen. And while you're waiting, be a ho!

Q: Do you think it's possible to love your spouse but also want to be with someone else?

A: Sure, but what do you mean by "be with someone else"? It's natural to fantasize about being physical with another person, or to wonder what another relationship might be like. Those thoughts are not crazy. But if this goes beyond fantasy, if you're thinking that this someone else is a way out of your current situation, then we need to be having a bigger conversation.

Q: Each guy I meet is more boring than the next! I just want someone with a good personality. Help!

A: As someone who has dated many men, I agree. Most of them are boring. Have you tried women? I have, and I don't like it. If personality is what's important to you, then set that intention and Mr. Right will come along when the time is, in fact, right.

Q: I think I have a thing for my best friend, who also happens to be my upstairs neighbor in my New York City apartment building. Should I risk the friendship and let him know how I feel?

A: My philosophy on dating friends is that if you're gonna shoot your shot, you've got to know you might be shot down. You've got to be willing to lose that friendship in your quest for love. Is this friendship worth risking? And you mention that you live in New York City. Consider this: Is a mediocre man really worth losing prime real estate?

Q: A friend of mine is cheating on her husband, and now she says she's in love with the other man. What should she do?

A: What should *she* do? I think the question is what should *you* do? And what you should do is sit back, be quiet, and let your friend make all the mistakes she needs to. This is not your fight. If my friend is out there being a ho, I'm going to sit back, say "That's my friend being a ho," and be there for them if and when it doesn't work out.

Q: I've been dating a guy for two months and I already want to walk down the aisle and have babies with him. Am I out of my mind?

A: I have a feeling you're not thinking rationally. Have you ever heard of being dickmatized? Let's wait to meet the family before we decide we want to put a ring on it and pop out some crotch goblins.

CHAPTER SEVEN

Dance, Dance, Evolution

Although I was obsessed with *TRL* as a kid and taught myself the choreography of Britney, Janet, Christina, and NSYNC, I didn't take my first actual dance class until after I graduated high school.

I met my friend George—the same one who suggested the Broadway Dance Center internship—during the summer after my senior year, when we were costarring in a production of *Footloose* at the Community Theatre of Greensboro. George was a year older than me, with all the wisdom of a man who'd completed two semesters of college. When he told me that if I wanted to be in musical theater I needed to be taking ballet, I listened. I enrolled in free beginner classes at a Greensboro community center, found ballet shoes for my giant feet, and showed up on my first day ready to work.

There I was, a six-foot-two eighteen-year-old man taking class alongside twelve-year-old girls. I was the only male in the room, and wore boxer briefs under my ballet tights, because that seemed like as good a choice as any. Little did I know that my junk was flopping every which way. During one of the first classes, my teacher pulled me aside. "Your crotch is very visible," he said. "You can't have your junk out there with all these young women. Get yourself a dance belt."

What the fuck is a dance belt?

I soon learned that a dance belt is basically a thong that presents and contains your crotch in a very practical way. Live and learn! But listen, sometimes you gotta put yourself in embarrassing situations or uncomfortable spaces to get what you want, and I did that. I wasn't at the same skill level as people my age, who'd been taking dance their whole lives. So, yes, I was a foot taller than my classmates, but if I wanted to train, it was going to have to be with the tweens. We stan a humble king who pulls himself up by the G-string.

I never got especially good at ballet—this big bitch is not exactly built like Natalie Portman in *Black Swan*—but I still took two or three classes a week that year (in between college classes and working thirty hours a week at Steak 'n Shake), and it sparked my curiosity about other forms of dance. I eventually signed up for a modern dance class and auditioned for UNC Greensboro master's students who were casting performers for their year-end showcase. I got a spot and dedicated whatever free time I had to rehearsing for these final performances. No shade, but the choreography was horrible—really, so lame. Still, it was an opportunity for me to dance, and I was committed. Later, during my Broadway Dance Center internship, I took eight classes a week. Two of them had to be ballet, and other than that I did mostly jazz funk and hip-hop, with some modern and lyrical mixed in. I even took a few tap classes, but I was really bad, and it gave me the worst shin splints. I don't fuck with tap.

Broadway Dance Center had a lot of major choreographers on their teaching roster, people who worked with big-time artists, and taking classes with them was how a dancer usually got their foot in the door. I was on the right path, but the next step was getting an agent. There are three major agencies that rep dancers—Bloc, MSA, and Clear—and each of them holds cattle call auditions once or twice a year. This is basically an open audition where dancers file into a room and perform in hopes of landing representation or getting cast in a specific role. In 2010, I attended my first agency cattle call. I was one of hundreds of dancers lining the halls of Ripley-Grier Studios in Midtown, praying for my big break. I wore my go-to look: drop-crotch sweatpants, white high tops, and a plaid flannel wrapped around my waist. As my audition neared, I took my spot in the studio. The room was thick with heat. So many dancers had already broken a sweat in there, it was basically a steam room. No matter! I performed my ass off—it was a hip-hop jazz funk routine—and somebody out there realized that I was talented enough, or good-looking enough (I think both?) to warrant representation. I signed with Clear Talent Group shortly afterward, and I was officially A Dancer.

It's funny, I feel like I should build this moment up more. After hustling my ass off and dreaming of being a performer in New York, here I was, doing the damn thing. I'd been signed! I was chosen! But I've always had a hard time savoring the moment or reveling in my success. When you grow up super poor, with nothing feeling permanent, it's hard to trust that any good fortune will last. Which is probably why my memory of landing an agent is not so much of excitedly thinking *"I've made it!"* as it is of nervously wondering *"What's next?"*

The other reason it was hard to fully feel the joy of having "made it" in the dance world was that, as a dancer, you are basically treated as live-action furniture. You are to be seen and not heard, and part of the job description is keeping yourself cool, calm, and collected. Getting too excited or fan-girly about a celebrity you're dancing for is considered unprofessional. It wasn't particularly hard for me to keep it together during that first gig for Countess Luann, because I didn't have cable. Bravo wasn't part of my repertoire (and maybe because that song, my god). Soon after that I got a gig dancing behind Stephen Colbert and Steve Carrell at Comedy Central's *Night of Too Many Stars,* an autism-awareness fundraising event hosted by Jon Stewart. It was my first televised dance gig, which would have been super exciting except it was a goofy number about Captain Sully Sullenberger and I played the goose who got stuck in the engine, which meant I spent my entire television dancing debut in a giant bird costume.

But as my career picked up, my projects did, too. I danced for Katy Perry, Pitbull, Nicki Minaj. The Katy Perry gig, which was at the Victoria's Secret Fashion Show, was especially exciting, because it was my first time dancing on TV where you could actually see my face, and it was the kind of jazz-pop dancing that I had trained for. The afternoon of the show, I arrived at the Lexington Avenue Ar-

mory in Midtown Manhattan and everything felt so major
with the glittery runway and cameras—it was a massive-
scale production. Not to mention there were celebrities
everywhere—the models walking the runway that year included Rosie Huntington-Whiteley, Adriana Lima, Ales-
sandra Ambrosio, Behati Prinsloo, and Lily Aldridge, and
people like Paris Hilton and Adam Levine and Adrian Gre-
nier and Vin Diesel were in the audience. I felt like I'd finally hit the big time. Katy herself was . . . well, she wasn't
mean, but she was fairly indifferent to the dancers. She
didn't really acknowledge us, but that was par for the course.
Over the next few years, I continued to book higher-profile
and more exciting gigs, and though on the inside I was having fun and was still totally giddy at the fact that I was actually getting paid to dance, on the outside I mostly stayed
quiet, speaking when spoken to, and turning it on for the
camera or the artist as instructed.

The one exception I can remember came in 2011, when I
performed with Nicki Minaj at the Victoria's Secret Fashion
Show. I was one of six backup dancers—I rocked a neon
yellow hoodie, a peace sign sweatshirt, and a beanie. A real
'90s fluorescent streetwear vibe. On the afternoon of the
show, we had just finished rehearsal and were waiting backstage while Maroon 5 did their run-through. My friend
Chris and I watched on the monitor. "Damn, Adam Levine
is so fine!" I exclaimed once the performance ended. "He
could get it!" My gay ass was being so extra, and as soon as
the words came out of my mouth Chris leaned in. "Don't
look now but he's right behind you," he whispered.

I don't know that Adam heard me, but I am not a quiet
person. That's fine. I said what I said. At that time, Adam

Levine *could* get it! Now, knowing what we do about his online behavior, I would like that statement removed from the record.

I met a few of my fellow Peloton instructors during those early dance days, too. In 2011, I was booked to dance at the Univision upfronts. The upfronts are a collection of presentations that TV networks do for marketers, usually in May, so they can see what will be on the schedule and decide where they want to put their advertising dollars. They can be pretty over the top, and that year, Univision had Pitbull performing. I was hired to dance in the aisles while Pitbull was onstage, and every dancer was paired with someone of the opposite sex. My partner? None other than Ally Love. We were the tallest dancers in the group—a stunning pair.

It was an exciting time, for sure, and it was incredibly satisfying to finally be a working dancer in New York. But don't be fooled. A career in the entertainment business comes with lots of rejection, and I was no exception. I auditioned for JLo a bunch—she'd come to the East Coast and audition dancers for various performances. I really fit in only one lane—"tall white guy"—and I was always up against the same other tall white guy. I wanted the JLo jobs so bad—not only because I was a huge Jennifer Lopez fan, but because dancing for her brought status and prestige. I wanted to be able to *say* I danced for JLo more than I actually wanted to dance for JLo, but I never got the opportunity. The jobs always went to the other guy.

And there were those extended trips I took to L.A., to see if I could get cast for bigger gigs on the West Coast. I auditioned for the Taylor Swift tour (no, I'm not a fan but

I wasn't too good to try to dance for her) and for Britney Spears's Las Vegas residency, which of course would have been a dream come true. I made it through the first day but got cut on the second, so I didn't get far enough in the process to actually see Britney in real life. That sucked, but worse was the actual rejection—being told I wasn't good enough. The hardest part about being a dancer is that you put all your worth into other people's opinions of you, and you get so lost chasing the dream that you start to forget it's something that brings you joy.

I knew that auditioning in L.A. would mean facing repeated rejection, but knowing that didn't make it any easier. I put so much hope and aspiration into those gigs, and I couldn't help but take the no's personally.

By the time I decided to stop trekking out to L.A. every month for auditions, I was beginning to rethink the dance career. I was twenty-six, and all my friends were progressing professionally. They were able to afford vacations and nice apartments and actual furniture, and I was tired of being broke. I got paid to dance, sure, but it wasn't a reliable income. I could plan ahead only as far as my next paycheck, because who knew when the one after that would come. Dance was the kind of hustle where I worked *so* hard without getting much in return other than a sense of pride and accomplishment. And those things are great—I love bragging rights—but they don't pay the rent, and they certainly don't fund a five-day vacation to Europe or South America. It was time to go back to day jobs.

The moment I decided to put a career as a professional dancer on the backburner, I began to appreciate how truly important dance was to me personally. I'm never more myself than when I'm on a dance floor. Going to clubs and listening to house music and soaking up New York night-life . . . all that is a part of who I am. Through dance I get to move my body and connect with people I care about and sometimes even connect with strangers. When that became something I could do entirely for fun, because it brought me joy and not because my self-worth and livelihood depended on it, I only came to love it more.

And so, of course it would happen that right when I thought dance was out of my professional life for good, it ended up serving me the most.

CHAPTER EIGHT

Ass in the Saddle

I don't believe in God. Most of the time, I believe we create our own luck, and that our good fortune is a product of hard work rather than being #blessed. We control how we seize opportunities, or how we react when things go wrong, and usually it's those choices that dictate the trajectory of our lives.

BUT! There have been occasional moments when, I'm telling you, I have manifested change right out of thin air.

After my attempts at making it in L.A. had fallen flat, I wanted to find a new career that felt like my own. So much of my dancing had been in service of someone else—that's literally what being a backup dancer is—and I was ready to occupy the leading role in my own life. So I decided to re-direct my energies toward making as much money as I could while I tried to figure out my next step. I didn't have a clear vision of what that new path would be, but I had an intention and the desire for change. I wasn't afraid to work for it, I just knew I wanted that work to be toward finding my light. And I put that energy into the world: I told my friends, I said it in front of the mirror, I announced it on Instagram. I wanted something new and something meaningful and something that would call on the skills that only I had to offer. Long story short, I was not shy about telling the universe that this bitch was ready.

But, a girl has to make a buck, so when I returned to New York for good in September 2013, I once again took on three jobs. I was working for a marketing company, I was cater waitering, and I was working at the Box. The Box was not (*is* not!) your average nightclub. It's a performance art space. While I was working there, they would feature unique burlesque acts throughout the night. One of them starred a trans woman, Rose, and she would be fully naked with her titties and her penis on display. Sometimes she would pee on people, other times she would stick glass bottles up her ass in front of the crowd. And all this was for the suit-and-tie set, where there had to be some transphobia, so she was pretty fierce, to be honest. (For the supremely curious, there's a documentary about her called *Miss Rosewood*.) There was also this campy number done to the Monica song "Don't Take It Personal (Jus One of Dem Days)" where a mime was painting while wearing a white suit, and then she started having her period and using the blood as paint. It sounds crazy, but it was one of my favorite numbers because people in the crowd did *not* see it coming. It was hilarious.

But then, in between these cabaret-type acts, there were singers who performed with backup dancers. A number of Peloton instructors were dancers at the Box at one point or another—it's where Jess King met her wife, Sophia, who was one of the singers there. My own role at the Box had nothing to do with dance, but everyone knew I was a former dancer because we'd all traveled in the same circles.

About six months to the day after I returned to New York and set my intention to find a new career, I got an email. It was forwarded from a colleague at the Box who directed the shows there. He'd gotten it from a friend from college, who at the time was launching the Peloton retail business. The email essentially said, "I'm looking for performers who are also into fitness. If you know anyone, reach out." My colleague at the Box forwarded it to a couple of us, and I took notice. A little alarm went off inside me. Ding ding ding! *I'm looking for something new, I'm a performer, I'd love to teach fitness instead of cater waitering.* I didn't know anything about Peloton as a company at this point—it was April 2014 and they had just launched. But I went to the gym daily and I knew how to perform, so this seemed like an opportunity I should at least investigate.

I can't say that I knew, when that email hit my inbox, that my life was about to change. But I'd spent enough time declaring my openness to career evolution that it seemed like it could be a sign. So I sent in my headshot and résumé and, within days, Marion Roaman, the former content director of Peloton, offered me an interview.

I will never forget the day I first entered the Peloton offices. This was before there was a studio. Within the office space, they had these black curtains blocking off a section of the room, and in that small space—referred to as "the closet"—was an instructor bike, with four bikes facing it. That was where they taught classes before the Twenty-third Street studio opened later that year. I can't remember who was teaching the day I interviewed, but I do remember that Jill Foley, wife of Peloton founder John Foley, was taking the class. She and three Peloton employees were the live riders for the day. It seems so DIY when I look back on it now, but at the time Peloton was just a scrappy start-up trying to establish itself. And that scrappiness was what made it great. I met with Marion for, I don't know, ten minutes, and then I met with John Foley, and about a half hour after I'd arrived, I had a job offer.

I know there are people with five-year plans who say *This is where I want to be and here are the steps I'll take to get there, and if I do X, Y, and Z, I'll get to this position.* Sometimes that's great and it works, but sometimes success—in career or in romance, wherever you are looking for growth or change—really is about being in the right place at the right time and being ready. And that's exactly what happened to me after grinding for years on end. Peloton pretty much fell into my lap.

I started my teacher training in April 2014. Jenn Sherman, Robin Arzón, Hannah Marie Corbin, and Jess King were instructors already. Hannah and Jess were also former dancers. It made sense that a number of us made that transition. Dancers are in tune with their bodies, they know rhythm, they know musicality, and if they've worked in a commercial setting, they know how to perform on camera. Also, for a lot of dancers (not just me) the jobs are inconsistent and you eventually become unfulfilled by the work, either because of the financial instability or because you're always working for other people rather than building your own brand.

Training back then included taking classes at Peloton, meeting with a mentor a few times a week, and getting a spin instructor certification through Schwinn. (Now we all have to have a National Academy of Sports Medicine, or

NASM, certification, which requires you to recertify every two years and is really time consuming, but people want their money.)

I'm not sure I'd go so far as to say I had a rocky start at Peloton, but it wasn't all smooth sailing either. Not only was I training to be an instructor, but I was still working at the Box and also cater waitering. (You can take the girl out of the hustle but you can't take the hustle out of the girl.) I'm not gonna name names, but someone who doesn't work at Peloton anymore almost fucked up my career there before it even started. As part of my training, my mentor—a former instructor—suggested I take classes from a successful male instructor at another cycling studio in the city. There were no men teaching at Peloton at that point, so she thought it would be helpful for me to see how it was done elsewhere. Seems reasonable enough. But somehow, this suggestion wasn't communicated to my boss, and a few weeks after I started scoping out male instructors around the city, my boss sent me an email. "Hey, Cody," it said. "I'm a little concerned that you aren't serious about Peloton because I haven't seen you taking classes in the studio. We need people who are committed to the company if this is going to work out." It probably went on a bit longer than that, but the takeaway seemed to be that I was fucking up, and the tone had real "shape up or ship out" vibes. I most definitely had a freak-out moment. *Am I about to get fired for following my mentor's advice?!*

I was pissed, and my first reaction was defensiveness. I wanted to write back and give a *per my last email*: "Listen, bitch . . ." Somehow I had enough wisdom to pause and calm down and put on my professional hat so that I could respond rather than react. (Mindfulness before I even knew its name.) I wrote back saying, "I think there has been a miscommunication; of course I am very committed to Peloton. I've been taking classes at other studios to get perspective on how male instructors teach, but I hope this doesn't affect my candidacy." She can be buttoned up when she wants to be! I was still only in training at this point, with no fitness teaching experience, so they had the upper hand. I was as professional as possible. My ass was on the line, so I kept it classy. It was the closest I ever came to lip syncing for my life, but we cleared up the confusion and I lived to train another day.

Before you launch as an official Peloton instructor, you have to do what's called a "community class," where you invite friends and family to take your ride. It's kind of a test run to see if you're ready to debut on the platform. It's nerve-racking, and don't be fooled by my cool confidence on the bike these days—I essentially failed my first one. It was not even close to good enough. Most of my friends had scheduling conflicts, so I didn't have any cheerleaders in the crowd and the energy was low. But more than that, I simply wasn't prepared, and it did not go unnoticed. The team in charge of debuting new instructors was like, "Nah, girl, you're not ready to launch. You gotta go back to the drawing board and figure this out." So I did just that. I spent the next two or three weeks getting back to work and doing my due diligence—I took more classes and observed more instructors, and generally upped my game so that when it was time for my second class, I was ready. For that one, a lot of my friends showed up. Quintin (who was in his blond eyebrow era) was there, Oscar was there, my friend Chris from the Victoria's Secret Fashion Show/Adam Levine incident, my friend Patrick—they were so supportive, and I had a better handle on what I was doing. The energy was bumping. The class was so good. It *felt* so good. I'd been told to step up my game, and I did. I was ready to launch.

By the time I debuted as an instructor in August 2014, the Twenty-third Street studio had just opened. I was at the bottom of the totem pole—I barely knew what I was doing—so I just tried to take as many classes as I could and learn as much as I could from the other instructors. I had three or four regularly scheduled classes on my teaching schedule, and whenever someone was sick or couldn't teach I tried to pick up their classes so that I could a) make the money (back then we were paid per class, now it's a salary structure) and b) get as much experience as I could. There was a point when I was teaching twelve, fourteen, sixteen classes a week. I literally don't know how I did it, because that is so taxing on the body. Sometimes that meant teaching two forty-five minute classes in a row—back then the bulk of our classes were forty-five minutes. It was a lot to take on. Now I teach about six classes a week, and that is plenty, thank you very much.

Like any start-up in its early stages, Peloton was kind of the Wild West back then. We were all making up our own theme classes, based on pretty much nothing but our interests. Every Friday night I would do an artist series, and this was before our official Artist Series was a thing. I would just say "It's Friday night, I'm doing a Beyoncé class!" and because we hadn't yet had any drama with music licensing, I'd go ahead and play "Single Ladies" and "Crazy in Love" and

"Ring the Alarm" and that was that. One December I decided to do an end-of-year ride that was a countdown of the top songs, so I singlehandedly reproduced (or tried to reproduce) all the album covers of those songs, but with me on the cover instead of the artist. It was all so scrappy, which I loved, because it forced a level of creativity from all of the instructors that helped define the company. We were all trying to figure out who we were as teachers and trying to grab as much of the market share as we could. But I was still new, so I spent a lot of time observing the instructors I thought were especially good. Robin seemed to have all her shit together and already had her kick-ass, sweat-with-swagger brand figured out. Jess King was so powerful with her words and so fun to watch.

The more I watched other successful instructors, the more I tried to incorporate their approaches into my classes. I road-tested so many different strategies, hoping something would stick, but none of it felt authentic to me. I'm not a badass trainer like Robin. I'm not sparkle and glitter like Jess King. I did a Tough Mudder with my friend Joe one weekend, and it was fun, but I'm not hardcore like that. I'm not trying to be hypermasculine or prove that I can conquer the elements. I'm perfectly content staying in the air-conditioning and leaving the mud to a beautiful face mask moment. Even when I started my mindfulness practice and meditation journey, I allowed that to influence my class a little too much. I'm certainly glad I did it, because it's how I got inspired to share more of my personal story publicly, but I think I let it become *too much* of my identity for a time. My classes became too serious and not as true to who I am.

I had no idea back then that being who I was *was* the secret sauce. After teaching for a bit, I somehow got privy to data that showed instructor popularity, and I was right in the middle. I wasn't the worst, but I wasn't the best. And I wanted to be the best. I wanted to be one of the top girls! I'm not usually a competitive person, but I've been aiming to be the best ever since that McDonald's drive-thru window. I am someone who wants to excel in all spaces. There's room at the table for all of us, and if I'm going to dedicate my time to something, I want to be great. So I used that Peloton data to understand what my audience looked like and what classes were doing well, and then I watched those classes to figure out why it worked and why it felt good. In my early days at Peloton, I watched every single one of my classes after the fact. Every single class! You know how painful it is to hear a recording of your own voice? How awkward it is to watch yourself on video? Now multiply that by a thousand. It was super fucking cringey. I HATED the sound of my voice. I thought it was so gay and so annoying (which, let's face it, it is), but I had to sit in that uncomfortable space to understand where my areas of opportunity were.

Together with my producer, I worked to be a better instructor and to gain more market share. My goal was to be consistent and make every class a good class, and that meant having an incredible intro, great programming, a good playlist—all the foundational pieces had to be in place. But here's the plot twist: I learned during all that studying and reflecting that what people responded to in my classes wasn't anything I'd learned from watching other instructors. People enjoyed my classes most when they were funny. They connected most genuinely to the wild things I said—me talking about food or nostalgia or my love for Britney Spears. Me laughing at the absurdity of life. And those were the things that were most authentically me. They weren't scripts I wrote ahead of time or came up with from watching others; they were ramblings that naturally spilled out of me when a song sparked a memory. They were silly one-liners that came as a reaction to a leaderboard name. These moments were all mine, and they were the antithesis of the typical fitness instructor persona. We think of perfect bodies, inspirational speeches, driven or tough instruction. Not only was that *not* me, but I realized that the stuff that *was* me was needed in the fitness space. My goal as an instructor became simple: Retain the consistent framework that I'd developed for each class and infuse it with my distinct brand of humor and fun. In other words, be myself.

With this new understanding of what my teaching should look like, I began to hit my stride. It was a self-fulfilling cycle. The more I was validated for being myself, the more joy I felt when I was teaching. (What more can any of us want than to be told that who we are is enough, and is exactly who we need to be?) The more joy I felt while teaching, the more fun and levity I could infuse into my classes. And the sillier my classes, the more riders showed up to take them, which validated my approach further. And round and round she goes.

I realized that people want to be entertained in the fitness space. They want to laugh and feel like a friend is there with them, encouraging them in the way that their actual friends would, because fitness can be scary. People feel shame because they don't know what they're doing, or they're embarrassed because they think the person next to them will judge them. If I could get on the bike and make fun of myself, or make a fool of myself, then maybe I could break down people's walls and help them feel a little more at ease.

A wonderful side effect of being myself and connecting with riders has been that occasionally, I've not only opened people's minds to fitness, I've also opened their minds (and hearts) to the LGBTQ community. A member once approached me crying after a Pride ride and told me that her child had just come out as trans. She was struggling with it, she said, but hearing me celebrate trans people and talk about my experience as a queer person helped her realize how important it was to simply love her child. I've had gay acquaintances in New York tell me that their sister, their aunt, their grandma takes my class, and that that person lives in a conservative town. There have been times when they weren't accepting or were downright homophobic, but then they fell in love with me or my class and it opened their minds and shifted their relationships. I've heard from closeted teens who've seen their parents take my class and felt a glimmer of hope watching a queer person accepted by a member of their family. *That* is my purpose. It's the most important thing about my job. It might feel like a silly thirty-minute bike ride, but it affects people and it changes minds. That's not the case for every rider—for some people it really might just be a lighthearted half hour and that's great, too—but if I'm reaching even just a few people on that deeper level, then my job is so much bigger than just fitness instructor.

But getting to this place took time. What I don't think

people understand about the pandemic era of Peloton and my seemingly overnight success is that it took six or seven years of hard work and failure and trial and error to give me the foundation I needed, so that when the lockdown hit and it was go time, I was ready. I had all those years to fuck up and figure shit out, and it's easy to forget that part of the story.

Around the same time that I figured out my teaching style, it occurred to my pesky pragmatic side—the same one that decided to work office jobs rather than just following the dance path—that I should take this opportunity as an employee at a start-up to sharpen my analytical brain and my business skills. Yes, I was a fitness instructor, but I knew I would get older and that I could get injured, so getting involved in the company in other ways added a layer of security. Not only did it feel like a way to be more successful at Peloton, but if something happened to me and fitness didn't work out, or if Peloton didn't work out, I would build muscles that I could flex at another job or on another adventure. At that point, Robin had been promoted to VP of fitness programming. From the jump she knew she wanted to be involved in the business side of Peloton, and I admired that. I wanted to follow her example. So one afternoon, while she and I were in the dressing room getting ready to teach, I pitched myself. "Listen, I've been here a little while," I said. "I know you're taking on this new role, and if there's any way I can be involved or if you see an area of opportunity for me, I would genuinely love to help. I'd like to grow." You've got to shoot your shot. I say that a lot, and for any of you wondering if I follow my own advice, here you go. I did it. And Robin listened. I'm forever grateful for that.

The first thing I took on for Peloton in a business capacity was research for our UK expansion. I went to London and took a bunch of spin classes and got perspective on what fitness looked like there, what their instructors were like, what kind of noncycling classes were popular. I worked hard across the pond because I had to prove myself. Sure, I'd found my groove on the teaching side, but Peloton was a business. They weren't going to give me a new role in the company if I didn't earn it. But I did like I always do, and eventually, I was made director of cycling, which meant I helped onboard and train new instructors.

My first assignment in that role was as point person for Denis Morton and Emma Lovewell after they launched. Robin onboarded them, but I was their support contact after the fact—helping them get settled, answering any questions, that sort of thing. (Side note: Emma didn't start working at Peloton until 2017, but I knew her from the dance world before that. One day I walked downstairs in the Peloton offices while she was interviewing, and I just started over-the-top gushing, like someone who is in on the bit. "Emma! Omg! You're here, you're amazing!" I really wanted her to get the job, and not that she needed my help— she didn't—but I wanted everyone to know I was a fan. Love her.) I did all the recruitment for the UK, which meant returning to England for a second visit. That one was tricky, because people there were still like, *What the fuck is Peloton?* I will say, I recruited both Ben Alldis and Leanne Hainsby. They were the first two instructors that I trained, so yes, I literally introduced them and now they are getting married. You can add matchmaker to my résumé.

My role included not just recruiting instructors but prepping them for their auditions and training them for launch. I can claim eleven instructors as the little birdies I launched from the nest: the UK and German cycling teams, Kendall Toole, Tunde Oyeneyin, Jess Sims on Bike Bootcamp, and Camila Ramón. Being the director of cycling was really important to me. I was an advocate for instructors with the production teams, and I learned a lot about how the business side of the company worked. I also loved that I could bring others into this amazing opportunity—I felt like I was paying it forward.

But the best part of being the director of cycling wasn't developing any specific business skill; it was having the chance to connect with so many of my fellow instructors. Of course we all get to know one another when we work together at Peloton, but I spent a lot of extended time with the instructors that I trained, which was an opportunity I relished. Of all the questions I get asked about working at Peloton, what riders always seem most curious about are the instructor friendships. "Are you guys *really* friends?" members will ask. So here's the tea: Instructors are people! We all have different relationships! At a base level, I truly believe there is a respect and genuine desire among all of us for everyone to be successful in their own way. But keep in mind, there are about fifty of us. The idea that I will be BFFs with all of them, or have a strong connection with all of them, is just not realistic. There are probably two handfuls of people that I have shared life experiences with, that I talk to often, and to whom I divulge whatever personal shit I'm going through. These people are my sounding boards and, in a lot of cases, we've been in the trenches together for nearly a decade. We have seen one another through so much, and when crazy shit happens, these are often the only people on earth who can understand what I'm going through.

Jenn Sherman is one instructor I'm super close with and talk to on a regular basis. She's like another cool mom to me. She'll probably kill me for saying that, but it's the truth! When I first started at Peloton, back when we were in the old studio, we had this tiny makeshift greenroom, and Jenn and I always snuck in there and locked the door so we could whisper about office gossip. We worked at a company that was always evolving, always changing, and that meant there was always something to dish about. It's good to have another person to debrief with. And we still do that! But she's also my biggest cheerleader. Jenn's always asking me "What's next? Then what?" and it's not from a place of pressure; she's genuinely invested in my success. In fact, she was the very first person I called to tell I was doing *Dancing with the Stars*.

If Jenn's my work-mom, then Alex Toussaint is the brother I never had. I've loved watching him grow up, and I may be older, but he's watched me grow up, too. We always hype each other up, we're always proud of each other, and we don't hold that encouragement back. We communicate and we push each other and sometimes we question each other, or at least we ask the right questions so that we can get to the right answers. That's been a super beautiful friendship for me. I've learned what he's been through as a young Black man trying to make it in this industry, and he's seen what I've been through as a gay man trying to find my light. There is this stereotype of homophobia within the Black male community, or just among men in general, so for him to start at Peloton at a young age and with a military school background and find this strong relationship with a gay man and support me through my journey, it's been really special to me.

My friendship with Robin Arzón has been interesting, too. She's someone with such laser focus that it can be hard to get her to be vulnerable or let her guard down, but even though she doesn't express it the same way I express it, I know she has nothing but love for me and support for me and is proud of me. Her success has motivated me, and she has pushed me professionally. Honestly, my relationship with Robin is a testament to the fact that we all communicate or show love in different ways. Whereas I'm an open book and super sappy and emotional and good with my words, she is good with support and hyping someone up and really showing up for people. Sometimes it takes stepping back and looking at the big picture to understand that all these different love languages are still love.

The casting at Peloton is intentional. We don't need two Ally Loves or two Alex Toussaints or two Emma Lovewells. We want diversity—not just in how the instructors look but in the stories they tell—and that's why when we branch out beyond the bike, those side gigs look different. I might be doing *Dancing with the Stars* while Jess Sims is hosting *College GameDay* and Robin is teaching a MasterClass and Tunde is hosting the Peloton podcast. We all fill different lanes, so we all take on different opportunities. It's an abundance mindset versus a scarcity mindset, and that's the way I want to live my life.

CODY'S DOS
AND DON'TS

DO be a ho. There's nothing wrong with being a ho. Be a ho! Be a ho all you want. Shake your ass, shake your titties, have fun. Do who you want to do. Just make sure it's consensual and respectful.

DON'T be that annoying-ass friend that's trying to split the bill by the penny. "I only had a water." Girl! Why'd you come? You just came for some water with lemon and Splenda? Next time, you won't be invited back. We're running up the bill and we're having a good-ass time.

DO be cold and lonely instead of warm and cozy with someone ugly. I don't need to see you all cuddled up next to some ogre because your ass was sad and you were scared of the rain coming down. Put on a flannel and a Lifetime movie and call it a wrap.

DON'T get involved with a coworker. You are bored, you see this person every day, you just got things going wild in your mind. You have so much trouble finding someone to date from the billions of people in this world that you have to pick Chad from finance? Please stop. On behalf of HR people everywhere, don't do it.

DO own it if you married for money. Just own it! "Yes, my man is busted, but I am driving to brunch in a G-wagon." Congratulations! You did it right.

DON'T wear flip-flops on city streets. New York? L.A.? Chicago? These streets are filthy! You're going to get back home with a dirty-ass foot and a thong line. It's disgusting! You don't love yourself.

DO get full-size candy bars on Halloween. Be that rich! Be the house every kid wants to go to! No cheap-ass candy, no fruit, no vegetables, and please, lord, no religious pamphlets.

DON'T date anyone who chooses Bowser as their *Mario Kart* character. If that happens in your presence? Bitch, run. Make a phone call, fake an emergency, get the hell out of there.

DO indulge in retail therapy! If you want to bury your traumas and discomforts in buying things, I condone that. Find some time this week to treat yourself. Just know the credit card bill will arrive at some point, so don't make any choices that will make the debt collectors come for you.

DON'T wear kitten heels. Just wear a flat! What is a one-inch heel going to do for you? Tell me.

DO put your leftovers in the oven. Skip the microwave. You deserve to savor the flavor. You deserve your reheated food to be crispy. You're worth it.

DON'T be trying to bring in fall at Labor Day. It's early September! I am still at the beach. Do not come at me with your PSL and your apple-picking and your knee-high boots. Not while I've still got my bathing suit on.

DO take one day and do it up for your birthday. ONE day. It is not a birthday month. Not a birthday week. You popped out on ONE day. There are 365 of them . . . we all get *one*.

DON'T throw a party with a cash bar. And if you do, don't invite me. You obviously are not in the place in your life to be hosting this function, and you are asking your guests to foot the bill for the alcohol? Time to reassess your decisions.

CHAPTER NINE

The Dating Game

I've dated a lot. A LOT. A lot a lot.

I've dated looking for love and dated to find something casual. I've had dates that I knew within minutes would go nowhere, and others I thought had promise and amounted to nothing. I've gone on dates with no hookups, and had plenty of hookups with no dates. And I have thoughts! There are things to say! I know we all have our own philosophies about how to live and how to mate, but you came for the sermon so please join your boo as he walks you through the ins and outs of love and romance, from that first meeting all the way to happily ever after, whatever your happy might look like.

The Stages

Let's start by identifying the stages of a relationship. There are more than you think, and I need to be sure we're all working from the same dictionary if we're really going to get into this. First, you are "seeing somebody." That means you've gone on a first date or maybe you've gone on a couple of dates. Maybe you've even hooked up. But it's not consistent, and you're definitely not exclusive. You're still feeling out if you want this to be a regular occurrence. When you're "dating," the dates and the hookups are all happening more consistently. It's not "Should we see each other again?" but "*When* should we see each other again?" Minor difference, but a critical one. Next, when you're "exclusively dating" it's just that. You aren't ready to seal the deal and be relationship-official, but you're dating only that one person and having sex with only that one person. Or, if you're not monogamous, you've openly discussed that and agreed to some ground rules. Next, when you're truly ready to explore a future with this person and they're the one for now, it's time to use those *boyfriend, girlfriend,* or, for my gender-neutral lovers, *significant other* labels. Then we've got *fiancé, partner, husband, wife* . . . I don't think I have to explain those.

The Date That Matters Most

This might not be the juicy content you came to this chapter for (that's coming, I promise), but I swear what I'm about to say is more important than any advice I have on kissing or first dates or whether you should pee in front of a partner (short answer: Sure, why not, but if you cross the line and take this to number 2, I'm judging). So here goes: Before you can be ready to date someone else, you have to be comfortable dating yourself. I know it might be annoying to hear this, especially if you just want to get boo'd up and find a warm body to spoon at night. But I'm looking out for you here, I promise. You have to know who you are—your values, your desires, your nonnegotiables, your strengths—before you can give your best self to someone else. I'm telling you this now to save you a lot of time and heartache later on. Most of us go through years of trial and error and failed pairings before understanding that we won't have a thriving relationship until we've embraced who we are. And those years can be painful. So I'm here to say, do the work now! The more comfortable you are with yourself, the less you'll need somebody else. The healthiest relationships are between two people who are independent and confident but *choose* to be together. When you *need* someone else because you're scared of being alone . . . well, that's not the best place from which to approach romance. It does not have the makings of a lasting relationship.

And when I say date yourself, I mean, truly, date yourself. Can you go to a dinner by yourself, and enjoy it? If you can't, why the hell should someone else want to go to dinner with you? Same thing with the movies, or travel. I love traveling alone. Of all my solo practices, it has strengthened my relationship with myself the most. All these activities that we so adamantly want companionship for, we need to get uncomfortable and do them with ourselves first. (You don't have to pause dating entirely just because you haven't figured out who you are. Dating and failed relationships can help uncover what we don't know about ourselves, but do some self-discovery before you start thinking about lifelong partnerships.)

How to Meet a Mate

When I am meeting men, I am still out here doing it the old-fashioned way. And by that, of course, I mean in the clubs. Listen, if you're a fan of online dating and it's working for you—congratulations. Live your life. People have different levels of social comfort, and everyone has so much fucking anxiety about dating and putting themselves out there that I say do what works for you. But I struggle with accepting dating apps into my relationship journey. I fully recognize that this is where society and technology has brought us, and there is no shame and no stigma against meeting your person online. There's nothing wrong with it! But it's not my fantasy. Call me a hopeless romantic, but there's still something special to me about that serendipitous moment when you lock eyes across a crowded room or spot someone sexy at the bar and you get that stomach-flipping heart-pumping buzz. There's something beautifully divine about two people being in the same place at the same time and having a connection. Leave me a Yelp review if this sounds bitchy but I've just never needed a romantic partner so badly that I wanted to turn to an app on my phone to find him. My time is valuable and it's better spent living life and having experiences than scrolling and swiping to find a date. (Side note: I don't understand people who write Yelp reviews. Do you have nothing else to do with your time? If you don't like a restaurant just don't come back! Honestly, I don't care about strangers enough to invest time into preventing them from going somewhere. But that's just me.) Being social, going to clubs, traveling, attending events—

these are the experiences that nourish my soul and create my joy, and I'm better positioned to find the right person when I'm in those spaces. When I'm alone at home on an app? She's crusty and dusty and not cute for anyone.

I'm talking exclusively about relationships and romance here. Hookup apps, on the other hand? That's a different story. You know I love to get slutty. There is never a bad time to be a ho. So, yes, I've met people on Grindr. I've met people on Instagram. We've had some fun escapades. Shenanigans ensued. But none of those rendezvous has ever amounted to anything serious, which feels right for me.

Also, what is it about setups? No thank you! No. Thank. You. I don't trust a single soul to set me up. I am so opinionated, there is no better person on this earth to suss out if a person is worth dating than me, myself, and I. And oh my god, straight women, stop thinking you know how to set up two gay guys! Just because you know two guys who are gay doesn't mean they are a match. You tell me he'll be great for me and then I show up at the restaurant and it's some gay who just moved to town? Oh no, ma'am. I know you think he's got a charming personality but that's not cutting it for me, babe. It's not enough. Straight women really do love a setup, which is hilarious to me because never in their lives would my friends meet someone and be like "Oh my god, you'd be a perfect match for Cody!" We just don't do that.

Setups also seem to center around this idea that being single is inherently bad. Like, *I need to set you up so we can fix this problem.* I don't know, to each their own, but that's not my philosophy.

I have met every boyfriend I've had in New York at a club. Well, that's not exactly true, but I've definitely encountered them all on a dance floor at some point before we were dating. I met my ex-boyfriend Matheus, who I was with for two years, in the locker room at the gym. But then I saw him out a bunch and we'd often go home together after a night at the club and eventually we became boyfriends. I first spotted Andrés, my current boyfriend, at the gym, too, but I finally shot my shot with him when we were both at the same rooftop party. There are a million ways to meet people and I'm not saying that any one is inherently better than another, but what works for me is living my life and moving through the world with an openness to connection. I'm not scoping out every room for my next date, but I'm open to possibilities.

First Dates

There are plenty of aspects of dating that I'm more than willing to accept are subjective—there's no "right" way to meet someone, as we've established. But first dates? Sorry, there is a right way and a wrong way, and if you are meeting someone for the first time over a nice long dinner, that is the wrong way. Dinner is a horrible idea for a first date. Just say no. When you decide to go out to dinner, you are committing to a much longer time than you might want to be with somebody who turns out to be a dud. Always start with drinks. And no, not coffee. I know people think that's the move but then your breath is going to be bad and what if you like this person and want to make out? First impressions matter. Don't try to kiss me smelling like Pike Place Roast.

I've made the mistake of doing the first-date dinner, so let me offer you a little cautionary tale. There was a guy I met multiple times at various clubs and parties, and we finally exchanged numbers and agreed to go to dinner. Beforehand, I met him at his apartment, and we made out for a little bit. I have to say, I highly recommend a reverse-date plan. Hook up *before* the date. Why not? You're not full, you're not feeling gross, you don't have bad food breath. I'm not trying to fuck or get fucked after having pasta! So I say make out, have sex, do what you're gonna do before the official date activities commence. But in this case, after the pre-dinner hookup, on the way from his apartment to the restaurant, this man pulled out a pack of cigarettes and started smoking. Da fuck?! Whatever, smoke if you want to smoke, but I knew from that moment that I wouldn't be able to date this guy seriously. Cigarettes? In 2022? Absolutely not. He immediately became so not hot to me. I wasn't attracted to him anymore, I didn't want to make out with him again, and I felt stuck. And then I had to sit through an hour-long dinner that I didn't want to be a part of. Nightmare. Hence why dinner is a bad first-date idea. I tried it so you don't have to.

And speaking of cigarettes, we all have deal breakers—those immediate red flags that signal a relationship will not be happening. Game over, do not pass go. Smoking is obviously on my list. Another big one for me is not tipping 20 percent or being a dick to customer service people. I once went on a date with a guy who left a 10 percent tip at the end of the meal and I was so embarrassed. Embarrassed! Humiliated! If someone shows you who they are, believe them, and this guy showed me he doesn't treat people well. Also, voting is mandatory. If you don't do your civic duty, you ain't getting no booty.

But in my experience, most of the time on a first date there are no major red flags. More often than not, the guys I go out with are nonsmoking, 20-percent-tipping, polite and politically engaged men. That doesn't mean we're going to be a couple, but that's fine. I can still have a good time. I can't believe I even need to say this, but it's just too easy to forget: Dating should be fun! Even first dates, with all their cringey awkward mishaps or bad kisses or messy goodbyes. If nothing else, you get a great story out of it. People put so much pressure on these encounters, but not every date is going to result in a love connection—in fact, most won't— and that's okay. It doesn't need to lead to something serious or even result in a second date. Sometimes you might not even be looking for something serious, and there's nothing wrong with that. Dating can just be dating.

Andrés and I first started dating in 2018, and we broke up for a bit in 2022 before getting back together. During the breakup period, after I took the appropriate amount of time to grieve and heal (see chapter 14 for my breakup TED Talk), I started going on dates not with the intention of see-ing someone seriously or trying to find a new boyfriend (I absolutely wasn't ready for that), but because I was at a place in my life where I didn't just want transactional sex. I wanted some level of connection and a little bit of intimacy to go along with the sex. Who woulda thunk it? But I wasn't dating in a serious capacity. I went on dates—first dates and sometimes follow-ups—to meet people and explore and have a good time. It's not supposed to be a chore.

Sex, Sex, and More Sex

In the dos and don'ts of dating, here is a major don't: Don't save yourself for marriage! Who the fuck still does that? You've got to test-drive a ride before you commit. You certainly need to know if he's good in bed and if the chemistry is there before you decide to sleep with no one else for as long as you both shall live. As we know, I've hooked up with men before the date has even begun, so I'm here to say that you should get it on sooner rather than later. And if he's not good in bed? Well, all I can say is that wouldn't work for me. To each their own, but for me that's so long, farewell, auf Wiedersehen, goodbye.

In my life I've slept with more men than I can share here. Not because I'm keeping it a secret but because I legit don't even know. I couldn't tell you my number if I tried, so please don't ask. I'd have to upgrade my data storage to keep track of that one. My friend Brian recently tried to compose a formula for how to calculate your body count if you're a gay man in a coastal elite city. Like, if it's one person per week in your twenties, then in your thirties it's two a month, then you subtract however many months you were in a monogamous relationship and double any months where you took a vacation or went to a Pride parade . . . maybe you'd be close? Stay tuned, the algorithm is a work in progress, but I think he's onto something.

One thing not accounted for in that mathematical equation is threesomes. Have I had a threesome? Sure. Of course. I have no problem with them. But an additive partner needs to be additive. If you and your boyfriend or girlfriend are having a threesome just to be spicy or to add heat to your relationship, hard pass. No single act is going to save a relationship—not a threesome, not a child, not a puppy, not an over-the-top social media declaration of love on Valentine's Day. A threesome should be focused on expression and exploration of the relationship. It should be an enhancing measure, not a rescue mission. But, really, if you want my most honest threesome advice—try it outside a relationship. Friends, strangers, whoever . . . but do it with someone who is not your partner if you want to keep things uncomplicated. Or, better yet, be the third wheel. It's always best to be the guest—you get all the attention and can make your exit whenever you want.

Finally, when it comes to sex, it all comes down to one thing—be great at it! Be a good kisser! Understand how and where to touch someone. Flirt with me, lube me up, follow my nonverbal cues. Use tongue but not too much. And get some practice in, with yourself or another consenting adult. Be a ho all you want. You won't be slut-shamed by me, that's for sure. But I *will* shame you for not being a slut.

DTR

My only concern when people go out in the world and tap as much ass as they want is that sometimes intentions get misaligned. While it's completely fine to date people with no desire for anything serious, you don't want to be misleading. I'm not saying you should announce your intentions the first time you share a drink. There's no reason to begin a first date with a big "I'm not looking for anything serious" moment, and no need to disclose if you're having three other dates that week. Go, have your three dates! Have the time of your life! But if you start seeing someone continuously or you can tell feelings are starting to develop on one side or the other, you need to be sure you're on the same page. If you're not, it's time to walk away. That can be really hard, especially when the sex is great. Or when you're lonely and enjoying the attention of someone who finds you attractive. Believe me, I know this. This slut has been around the block. But you need to be honest, with yourself and with others, about what you want and what you're capable of in any given moment. Don't be selfish. You might want to fuck other people, but you don't want to fuck *with* them. It's the Hippocratic oath of dating: First, do no harm.

Hopefully, if you're in a place where you want to commit to someone and take the relationship to the next level, they feel that way, too. And while you need to align on the basics—*Are we seeing other people? Are we both open to seeing where this leads?*—I don't think you have to rush to officially Define The Relationship. It takes time to know if you want to invest in someone for the long-term, and when you rush to have a big "What are we?" conversation, it's as if you're trying to ease your anxiety or feed your attachment style rather than get in tune with how you actually feel about a person. It's easy to mistake a yearning for security with a desire for an actual specific human being.

My relationship with Michael, the married man I dated despite knowing better, probably fell squarely into that category. I did not have my priorities straight in that relationship. Aside from the obvious baggage of HAVING A HUSBAND, this man wasn't very cute, he didn't have an incredible body, he was wildly insecure, and had countless mommy and daddy issues that he was processing in toxic ways (like cheating on and lying to his husband). He did have a big dick, which was definitely a factor for the pro column. Good D is good D, but good D doesn't make up for a complete lack of emotional stability. But I was twenty-four and I wanted a warm bed at night. What I should have done was taken a beat to slow down and examine *why* I wanted to be with this man. I could have saved myself a lot of heartbreak later on. But learn from my mistake, girl. Ask yourself: Why do I want to be with this person? Is it because I have feelings for them and I enjoy their company and I admire and respect them and they make me laugh? Or is it because I'm nervous about being alone and want to know that this person, *any* person, belongs to me? Let's all move away from the idea that we should love a partner as something that is *ours*, and remember that people choose to have us in their lives, so we should always be working to earn that spot.

All that said, I don't consider someone my boyfriend until we've addressed it head-on, which usually comes in the form of an adorable "Are we boyfriends?" moment. I've never gotten proposed to so I can't speak to that, but I always think the two most special times in a relationship are when you ask someone to be your boyfriend or girlfriend, and when you say "I love you." Both are so vulnerable and so risky that when it's confirmed or reciprocated, there's such giddiness and excitement. And there's a buildup to each of those moments that is special.

You know that early stage of a budding relationship, when there's all this nonverbal communication—the exchange of a look at a party, or maybe a shoulder squeeze

when you're out shopping? Those moments are so powerful. They express connection and reinforce a partnership
and they inch you ever closer to saying those four letters.
There's something so sweet and pure about that phase, when
you're ruminating on the idea of saying "I love you" and
you believe it's true but you're also not quite ready . . . but
still you really, really want to. It's a bit of a dance: You're
unsure but you want to let it out and you're trying to read
the other person to understand if this is the right moment.
And then it happens: You say "I love you," and they say it
back. Is there any better feeling? To be that open and honest
and vulnerable with someone and to have it received with
love and care and protection—it's transformative. Even me,
your resident petty, sarcastic, and possibly jaded gay who
can make a joke out of everything, even I have a soft spot
for how raw and real that time can be. If you don't, as my
therapist says, we should unpack that.

But listen, these moments are beautiful because they are
authentic. Not because they happen quickly or on anyone
else's timeline. So don't rush it. As far as I'm concerned,
there is no reason to fast-track any of it—not the boyfriend/
girlfriend/theyfriend conversation, not the "I love you"
moment, not moving in together or whatever important
steps come after that. Because if you're putting yourself on
a timeline, you've already shifted your focus from honoring
your feelings to checking a box. By letting the necessary
time go by, you will be more in tune with yourself and more
in tune with the relationship, which will give you the requi-
site comfort and grounding to savor those vulnerable moments and really be present. Because they only happen once.
You'll say "I love you" a lot, but nothing will be like that

first one. So enjoy the buildup and savor the anticipation. It's like sex. You want foreplay. You want to enjoy everything that leads up to the orgasm. Please, take your time.

The Social Network

Okay, so you've got yourself a significant other, or you're dating someone and things are getting more serious. My PSA for the day: You are going to, at some point, have to meet that person's friends and, bitch, you better be ready to TURN IT OUT. The friends are so important. You want to fucking impress the friends. Be fierce. Be on your A-game. Give them your undivided attention. This is where I shine. In every serious relationship I've been in, I have won over the friend group. If I am getting introduced to someone's friends, I am ready to give a show, baby. You are not gonna catch me off guard and I am not failing this test. I know how to work a fucking crowd. I always home in specifically on the Best Friend. That person is my target. I really lean into whatever common interests we have and try to connect over those. One of those interests, of course, is the person I'm dating, so I like to gently poke fun at that person with their friends. I would never be cruel, but it's always good to join in for a little light teasing to show you know what's up, that you like their friend in spite of, or because of, their adorable quirks. Poking fun demonstrates that you're not too precious and that you can hang.

The truth is, you should be doing more work trying to impress the friends than trying to impress the one you're with, because these people are going to be the judge and jury. And they will absolutely come down with a verdict!

I've seen what happens when you don't put in the effort. Take a recent weekend in Fire Island. A group of us were in a share for the summer, and one of my friends decided to bring his new boyfriend for a couple of days. I'd already met this guy a few times out in the city, and it never seemed like he particularly cared about winning us over. But when we found out he was coming to Fire Island, we tried to give him the benefit of the doubt. Maybe he was shy! It can be hard to be an outsider infiltrating a tight group of outgoing gays.

Fire Island is a place where there is limited to no internet. You're sort of forced to unplug and engage in analog activities like puzzles or reading. One of my friends brought a bunch of nail polish to the house, so one night we decided to gather in the living room for nail painting and drinking and gossiping. A perfect opportunity to get to know our friend's new beau, or so we thought. Well, he wasn't having it. While we were having fun and chitchatting, he was sitting in the corner playing Pokémon and completely not engaging. His behavior sent the clear message that he did not think we were worth his time, and I was turned off enough that I ended up calling him out. "Didn't anybody teach you any manners?" I said. "You're being extremely rude."

I was out of line, I know, but I was fed up with the attitude, as if the people in his boyfriend's life didn't warrant any effort. He reminded me of one of those children at an adult restaurant, where the parents have to give the kid an iPad just so he can sit politely for an hour.

Was there a group text later debriefing this guy's performance? Of course! There always is. So if you are meeting the friends, take that into account and show up ready to slay. Leave the Pokémon at home.

On the flip side, if you start dating someone and you do a meet-the-friends moment and the friends are wack? That's a red flag. If you can't connect with someone's friends — and I'm not talking about one specific person, I mean if you don't vibe with the group as a whole — it's probably a sign that this relationship isn't right for you. A person's friends are a reflection and extension of who they are, so use any interaction to gather intel about the potential future of the relationship.

And when it's time to introduce your new partner to your friends, take their opinions into account. If you are into someone and your friends don't like them, it doesn't mean you must automatically kill the relationship, but at least take pause. I had a friend of a friend who started dating a new guy, and my friend had a hunch that something was off. He was pretty clear with his pal that *Hey, I don't like this guy, he's not a good match for you.* His friend ignored the warning, which was his prerogative, and ended up dating this man for three years. Then the guy left him for some sugar daddy in Miami, and it was a real don't-say-I-didn't-warn-you situation.

Also, your love interest should meet the people who are important to you *in person.* YOU DO NOT NEED AN ENTIRE SOCIAL MEDIA POST INTRODUCING THE WORLD TO YOUR BOYFRIEND. Sorry to yell, but oh my god. No one needs to announce their relationship to the world just like no one needs to showcase all the Pinteresty ways they accomplish their couple goals. Gross.

If you are writing a massive post about how much you love somebody, just tell them! You don't need to be performative. You shouldn't need other people's validation to affirm your feelings about your relationship. Have those conversations *with your partner*! Make sure *they* know how special they are. Why would you need Pam from accounting to "like" a photo to know that your relationship is strong? I guarantee that the people with the four-paragraph Instagram posts are not having deep, meaningful conversations with their partners about how much they love them. They are ignoring them while they post on Instagram. I see you. We all see you.

Grand Gestures / Gifts / Holidays

Performance, in general, is clearly not my favorite when it comes to romance. And this comes from a performer! Some things are better kept between two people. Take grand gestures. I know they've been romanticized by pop culture, and plenty of you reading this have dreamed your whole life of having a man show up at your door with cue cards announcing "To me you are perfect." But in real life, anything over the top just feels so fake. Grand gestures always seem to be for the person *doing* the thing to feel good about *themselves* and not really about showing love or adoration to the person on the receiving end. For example, I *cannot stand* someone who sings for their partner in public. Straight men, put down the acoustic guitars. This is not romance. This is you thinking you're a singer so you want attention. It is the cringiest thing ever. I feel the same way about brides doing dance performances at weddings. Hot take, I know, but I'm always like, girrrrl. You took jazz and ballet in middle school and now you want one final stage. We get it. Your time has passed.

It's not that I reject all gestures of love or kindness. I believe in gestures that express care and consideration of the person on the receiving end, and that usually translates to a small thing rather than a big one. A good partner is intuitive and pays attention to what their partner needs or what they want that they haven't bought for themselves. Maybe they're stressed at work so you order them a delivery of their favorite food. That's thoughtful! It's personal. It says, *I see what you're going through, I'm here to help.* One of my favorite gifts I've ever given was, on paper, pretty random. When Andrés and I met, he was living with a roommate in an apartment that was quite bare. My friend Miles, an interior designer, has always told me that lighting makes a space, and the lights in Andrés's apartment were pretty shitty. So for Christmas that year I got him this lamp that looked like a red cube but it made this gorgeous light in his home and really elevated his space. He loved that gift.

Andrés and I share a love of interiors, so he has bought me some vases that sit on my coffee table, and this ceramic art deco piece that I love—all stuff that I wouldn't have necessarily purchased myself but that make my space feel homier and remind me of our shared passion for design. These gifts are meaningful; they aren't just tokens because it's Christmas or Valentine's Day. I could do without Valentine's Day entirely, to be honest. I'm not anti, exactly, but who needs it? I don't like when things feel mandatory. And I hate roses. If anybody gives me roses it's like, *Oh, wow, you put no fucking thought into this whatsoever, knowing damn well my favorite flower is a hydrangea! Thanks a million!*

New Year's Eve is another one, while we're on the subject of holidays. There's all this pressure to kiss someone at midnight and ultimately all you can do is hope to not be standing next to someone ugly when that clock strikes twelve. My personal philosophy is to stay at home for the ball drop, go to sleep, and then find a daytime party on January 1. A bottomless mimosa bar, perhaps. But on December 31? Everyone is a mess, it's so cold in New York City, and if you can't find an Uber you're going to be miserable. That said, if you do go out, kiss as many people as possible, including your friends. My holiday of choice—and the best for anyone in the dating world—is Halloween. You get to dress like a slut and act like a mess. What more could you want? Of course, that's only one day. I'm not sure what the excuse is for the other 364, but whatever. Being a ho is a lifestyle (trademark pending).

The Hard Times

Relationships are not all cuddles and heart emojis. Obviously we hope there's more good than bad, but even the healthiest and happiest relationships hit hard times. Challenges are not an indicator of a doomed relationship. How you deal with those challenges, on the other hand, is telling. When my friends come to me with relationship woes, they're usually talking about one of two things: jealousy or boredom.

Jealousy is an ugly emotion, but we've all felt it. I want to sit here and say *Don't be jealous, you are THAT bitch*—and I believe that!—but I know it's not that easy. So instead of telling you not to feel your feelings, I want to encourage you to pay attention to the moments when envy or insecurity creep into your relationship and investigate what they might be telling you. Usually it's a clue to something bigger—fear or discontent, perhaps. I've definitely had moments where I felt insecure because my partner was making time for friends or going out with colleagues when I wanted him to save his time for me. But I had to ask myself, *What am I scared of?* Because the truth is, you *shouldn't* be spending all your time together, and, in a healthy relationship, time spent apart is time spent enriching yourself so you can bring that enriched self back to the relationship. Even if your lover is going somewhere they can flirt with someone, when a relationship is strong you'll feel confident that either they won't flirt, or that they will (with your permission) and it will be harmless. Flirting is fun! There will absolutely be scenarios in which your partner is alone and someone finds them attractive and starts to flirt with them. And, listen, we all like attention. We all want to feel hot. It's natural to reciprocate that energy—you will (and should) do the same thing when someone comes at you with their fun and flirty best. But being okay with any of this takes trust. That's really what all jealous interactions come down to. If you find yourself haunted by the idea that your person is going to talk to someone else or smile at someone else—if one flirty interaction with another human being is going to destroy your relationship—well, honey, you've got bigger problems.

If jealousy comes from distrust and a fear that we don't know what the other person will do, boredom is just the opposite. Our romantic relationships fall into a rut when things get routine and predictable and the proverbial spark is gone, but that usually happens only when we aren't giving the relationship the proper attention. Your relationship with a partner is exactly like your relationship with yourself—you've got to make time for it and dedicate energy to it and not take it for granted. It's too easy to go into autopilot, which results in monotony and resentment. And I get it, we're busy. We're juggling three jobs and trying to work out and keep up with friends and see our therapist and take care of parents. I know this because I just outlined my own life. But we still need to make time for the things that are important to us, even when they seem like they're in a steady state or run like a well-oiled machine. Even well-oiled machines need maintenance or they start to fall apart. Did I just make a car analogy? Okay! Butch!

As is the case with most problems, addressing a relationship rut starts with communication. I know, this is my answer to so many of the conundrums outlined in this book. But isn't that nice? Ninety-nine percent of relationship problems, of all kinds of problems, can be solved by having challenging conversations. If you can sit down with your partner and address your concerns and also discuss what's going well and what you want to keep doing, you're already a step ahead.

But sometimes, yes, actions speak louder than words. If you want to keep your relationship spicy, you gotta show up! Make sure your partner knows you want them. Maybe that means sending dirty text messages. Maybe it's nude photos. But be sexy! And I'm not talking about six-pack abs or low-cut shirts. Sexy is a VIBE, not a specific look. Be confident, be strong. Know what you want and go after it.

I know there's a theory that the secret to keeping the spark alive is to always retain mystery in the relationship, but I don't know. Whenever someone gives that advice, it seems to me like they're trying to find a more polite way of saying *Don't fart in front of each other.* But really? No farting? I can only speak for myself, but I've got a lot of gas— there's no way I could go through an entire long-term relationship hiding it. Those moments when you need to fart and you actively try not to are a lot of work. And listen, it's always awkward the first time, but then the floodgates are open and you can really be yourself. I'm okay with this. I feel the same way about peeing in front of each other. It's not a sign you are too comfortable—what is *too* comfortable anyway? Shouldn't we be comfortable with the people we love? (I will say, sometimes I sit down to pee, because I'm lazy as fuck, and something about doing that in front of a partner just doesn't compute. I heard that Meghan Trainor and her husband have his-and-her toilets so that they can shit together, and I don't subscribe to that. Let's keep shitting in front of each other to a minimum, okay?) But the point is, generally, I don't love that "mystery" advice. I say let this person know the full you, and love the full you.

Don't Settle, Be Single

No matter how much effort you put into getting through the hard times in a relationship, there may come a moment when you have to make a decision: *Is this relationship for me?* If I had to distill all my relationship advice down to three words, they would be: Do. Not. Settle. Don't do it! Know how hot you are. If the person you're with isn't matching your hotness, you're settling. It's as simple as that. And hotness isn't about looks—it's about how you carry yourself. You should feel sexy inside and out, and if the person next to you in bed isn't living up to your fierce and flirty energy—that's settling. If you've got an ogre in your bed but you're keeping him around because you want a warm body to keep you company—that's settling. I am tired of watching hot girls date booger-ass guys. It really bothers me. But that's what happens when we settle. Settling gets you an ugly boyfriend. That's just how it works; I don't make the rules. And you are too sexy and too grown to have some ugly-ass boyfriend.

You know what's better than settling? Being single. Having the freedom to do what you want on your own terms is liberating, as is being able to make spontaneous choices without taking anybody else's plans or feelings into account. If you're so wrapped up in the need to be in a relationship that being single gives you night terrors, reframe it as being in a relationship with yourself. Love the one you're with, boo. I wish more people would strive to spend young adulthood being single and not look at it as a punishment. It's freedom and discovery! It's a gift! Your presence is a present. You got all the good wrapping paper. You got that big-ass bow. You're the whole package, no accessories required.

CHAPTER TEN

Role Reversal

When I left North Carolina and moved to New York, my mom pretty much survived on the kindness of friends and strangers. By then she and Donald were done for good, so she lived with various friends for the next ten years, either not making an income or living on disability.

I visited her a few times a year—usually taking the Chinatown bus from New York to Greensboro. Oh, the Chinatown bus, that shit is crazy. It's a ten-dollar bus ticket (or it was back then) that takes you from one city's Chinatown to another's. It's cheap, but it's cheap for a reason. It's run-down, hot, and you basically have to cross your fingers that you'll get a seat and make it to your destination. But it got me where I needed to go, and a couple of times a year my mom would take it north to visit me. That's more or less how we proceeded for a while. We were still close, and we would chat on the phone a lot—my mom has always been a great listener and, despite her own messiness, she gives great advice—so I always kept her up on what was happening in my life.

At the same time, I knew that I had left North Carolina for a reason. Most of that reason was to follow my New

York dream, but it was also an opportunity to set some boundaries between my mom and me. I didn't have the vocabulary to say that outright, but I knew I needed some level of separation in order to establish myself and my independence. It was complicated, because even when you know you're making the right choices, they're not always easy. I knew I needed to be on my own, but I also knew that being on my own meant washing my hands of my mother's needs for a bit. It felt selfish, and that was hard. Being selfish isn't always a bad thing, but it comes with a cost. For me, that cost was a level of guilt I had to accept and live with. I still sent my mom money from time to time (money that I didn't have because I was broke, too), or paid for something she needed on my credit card. And I've always paid her phone bill—that didn't stop when I moved. I wasn't about to cut her off entirely.

A few important things happened over the next decade, while I was trying to make it in New York and my mom was trying to get by in North Carolina. First, I got my job at Peloton and started earning a decent and steady income. Second, and more important, I started doing a lot of work on myself—going to therapy, practicing mindfulness and meditation, and really trying to unpack a lot of my own baggage. I truly don't think I knew, before starting therapy, that a lot of my personal issues surrounding trust and security and attachment were rooted in my upbringing. I sought out therapy not because of anything going on with my mom but because I'd gone through a bad breakup. Still, as anyone who has ever been in therapy knows, a lot of the behaviors that inspire us to seek help, the behaviors we often want to change in ourselves, stem from shit that happened in our childhoods that we have yet to process. My therapist helped me look at moments from my past in a new light. Driving down the streets of California with rain splashing in the car? Maybe that was super fun, or maybe it was my mom in a manic phase. Actually, it was probably both. When my mom lashed out at me and threw a pizza across the room? That wasn't me having done something wrong, that was my mother's bipolar disorder taking control. It was still a scary memory, but now it had more context.

Beginning therapy and really digging into my past was not easy work. There were a lot of tears and I had to face a lot of anger and resentment that I'd been burying and denying. But I also learned to make space for compassion and forgiveness—toward my mother and toward myself. The first step toward letting go of hard feelings is to acknowledge and accept those feelings, and I did that. I also learned to recognize some patterns in my relationship with my mom, which made it much easier to move on from them. What I came to realize was that I would always have to be the caretaker in our relationship. I had spent years being bitter and frustrated that my mother couldn't get her shit together or that we went without so much when I was younger. But through self-work and self-exploration, I finally accepted that, yes, there was a lot of trauma in my life. I went through a lot of shit no child should have to face. But I also came to accept the simple truth that my mother needed to be taken care of. There was no way around it. She just didn't have the capacity to be entirely independent. I could keep pushing against that truth because I didn't want the responsibility, but that wasn't going to change anything. It would only mean holding on to resentment while my mom got older and potentially sicker. (At this point she was not only a former addict, which took a toll on her, and dealing with bipolar disorder and anxiety, but she'd also been diagnosed as diabetic and wasn't taking great care of her physical health.) Rejecting my role as caretaker might result in less work for me, but it would mean regretting that I didn't have a more loving and compassionate relationship with the person who gave me life. It also meant I would have to live with that regret if things took a bad turn.

In 2018, as I was working toward becoming a meditation instructor, I went on a retreat where I spent a lot of time focused on the idea of imperfect care. We are all here because somebody took care of us—somebody fed us and changed our diapers and tried to make sure that we were alive. That care may have been messy, but that person's intention was to do the best that they could with the tools at their disposal, and without that care—without that kindness or support or whatever it was they provided—we wouldn't be here. We wouldn't exist. That idea was super powerful for me. I spent a lot of time on that retreat thinking about my mother, having gratitude for her, and recognizing her mistakes while not letting them overshadow the purity of the fact that she tried to provide as best she could. It's easy to pass judgment on her actions, and I did so for a long time, but the more I meditated on it, the more I came to understand that she did her best under hard conditions. She was facing addiction. She had health problems. She was battling her own demons. Addiction is a disease. Mental health problems are complicated. Gaining that perspective was transformative for me, and ultimately for my relationship with my mother.

Soon after that retreat, I decided to move my mother out of North Carolina, so that she could be closer to me. She was living with a friend outside of Greensboro, and for various reasons, that living situation had gotten chaotic and stressful. Every time I talked to her, it was clear she was unhappy, and I was finally at a place where I not only *wanted* to take care of her, but I could afford to. I had been living with Quintin in Brooklyn for a few years at this point, and I was planning to move to Manhattan to live on my own for the first time in my adult life. Instead, I decided to forgo the move so that I could afford to bring my mom to the Northeast. I traveled down to North Carolina to pack up her belongings and relocate her to an apartment I'd rented in Nutley, New Jersey. New York City just seemed like too harsh a landing from rural North Carolina, which is where she'd been staying, and Nutley was only about an hour away.

I wish I could say that once my mother was closer, everything was magically fixed, but real life is messy, and as with most things, taking care of my mom got harder before it got easier. Her first few weeks in New Jersey were chaotic as fuck. I realized pretty quickly that she didn't have a good handle on her medical issues. I think her doctors in North Carolina were prescribing her meds in order to check a box rather than giving her any sort of personalized care. She was on Ambien for sleep, lithium for her bipolar disorder, and plenty of other drugs, and I don't think she had a grasp on what each medicine was for or how they interacted with one another. I didn't really have a sense of it either, until she'd been in New Jersey for a few weeks and we had our first real wake-up call.

My mother moved to Nutley on October 1, 2019. Every Wednesday after work I'd get a Zipcar and drive out to check on her. I'd take her to Target and to the grocery store, and just generally use the time for us to catch up and be together. On Wednesday, October 30, I followed the same routine—went to Nutley, did the errands. When I got back to my mom's place, I started working on a playlist for an upcoming class, and she told me she was going to take her dog, Ginger, for a walk. A good amount of time went by, and I started to wonder where she was. Walking the dog was usually a quick outing, but eventually Ginger came prancing into the bedroom where I was working and hopped on the bed next to me. She still had her leash on, which was odd, but I didn't think much of it until even more time went by and I still hadn't seen my mother. *What the fuck is going on? Why is the dog here and she isn't?* Something was definitely up, so I went outside and started calling my mom's name. Nothing. Of course, at this point, I was freaking out. After fifteen minutes of looking, I called the police. Luckily they found her on a side street. Apparently, my mother had taken an Ambien before she took the dog for a walk, and when the Ambien kicked in, she passed out on the street. By the time the police found her she was wet and cold and basically nonresponsive. It was a lot, to say the least. I always remember the date of this fiasco because I canceled my Halloween ride so I could be with her in the hospital. This was when I realized that I had to take responsibility for getting her health in order. The status quo was not okay.

The second and final wake-up call came a couple of months later, in December, while I was on a vacation in Brazil. I was having trouble reaching my mom while I was away, and when I did she sounded very . . . not herself. Something was definitely off. There had been times before when I'd had trouble getting ahold of her, but it was clear to me that something was different this time. I contemplated coming home early from vacation, and I'm still not sure if that would have been the "right" thing to do—it's impossible to know how different scenarios in our past might have played out. What I do know is that when I finally got home and went to check on her, I found the apartment a fucking mess and my mother in her bed naked, responsive but barely. She was completely unaware of what was going on around her, and she had lost control of her bodily functions. It was chilling. I had returned home to my mother having a psychotic breakdown. It was completely overwhelming. I wanted to take care of my mom, but I also worried that I was in over my head. I didn't know anyone else my age who was taking care of a parent like this, so I didn't have anyone to lean on or ask for help. It occurred to me in that moment that I hadn't realized what I was signing up for when I moved her to New Jersey. I felt defeated, exhausted, and frustrated.

It turned out that my mom had become lithium toxic. Basically she had too much lithium in her blood—whether it was from taking too much or being prescribed the wrong amount or from taking it for too long, that I don't know. But combined with not taking her insulin properly, the lithium toxicity—which is just the medical term for a lithium overdose—had disastrous effects. She ended up staying in the hospital for two weeks. I'd always known that my mother had mental health struggles, but I'm not sure I knew the extent of them until that episode. I'd had trouble viewing it from a lens of compassion. A part of me lumped her mental health and her addiction issues into one big pile of *Here's this shit that follows my mom around; why can't she fix it?* But during those two weeks, I came to understand that her depression and bipolar disorder and anxiety meant she had far less control over her behaviors and actions than I thought.

I am a person who doesn't suffer from any mental illness, and I still have sad moments and anxious moments. I still lose control and make mistakes. There's so much mental and emotional gymnastics to do to just be a human in the world, and to be the good person or partner or friend we want to be. When that is compounded by severe emotional dysregulation, there are so many more hurdles to acting in the ways you want to. Getting a firmer grasp on that helped me understand why my mother was the way she was, and why she couldn't do more to provide for us when I was a kid. Once I knew better, I could do better. I found her a good psychiatrist and a good primary care doctor, and things vastly improved from there. As always, I figured it out. It was really fucking hard, but I did it.

Today my mom lives in Brooklyn, in an apartment I bought for her about four blocks away from mine. By July 2020, driving back and forth between New York and New Jersey was becoming too much for me. I spent a lot of time during the pandemic running errands for her and trying to make sure she stayed safe, and earlier that month, her downstairs neighbor's air fryer caught fire, and the whole place went up in flames. It was the final straw—the kick in the ass I needed to uproot my mom one last time and officially move her to Brooklyn.

At this point, I really do want to provide for her and take care of her. And I feel so fortunate that I have the means to do so. But it's a constant and complicated balance of figuring out how much I need to do for her and how much I should make her do for herself. The reality is, the "need to do for her" bucket is getting bigger and bigger. There are days when I think I live up to my obligations as her son and other days when I worry I'm not doing enough. I get so bogged down with the responsibilities of my own life that I worry I'm not putting action behind the intentions I set when I moved her out of North Carolina. It can be easy to go into autopilot, making sure she has food and a roof over her head and the medication she needs, or calling her an Uber so she can get to doctor's appointments, but then I forget to have the more intimate or fun moments with her—which of course are the moments you cherish far more than the to-do list of parent caretaking. But that's the endless internal struggle. Overall, I try to give myself a little bit of grace and remember that I'm giving her the most that I can.

The other day, I was at my mom's place, just sitting and chatting with her, and out of nowhere, I looked into her eyes and started to cry. Her health continues to decline, her struggles have gotten more challenging, and I just want her to know that I am there for her. I will take care of her. In that moment, I decided to just say how I felt, which, as we all know, is a lot harder than it sounds. "I love you so much, Mom," I said. "I don't want you to worry—I've got you."

I realized that we have to love our parents like they are going to die, because they are. I know that sounds morbid, but it helps me to remember that our time with the people who raised us is limited, and that it's important to savor it. My mom didn't know quite how to respond to my sudden outburst of emotion. She got a little emotional herself and just said, "I know you'll take care of me, but I don't want to be a burden." When I tell her I love her she usually says something to the effect of "I know you do because if you didn't love me you wouldn't have put up with all my shit for such a long time." It's not exactly a thank-you, but I know it's her way of communicating gratitude. I think she does feel some level of regret or sorrow that she couldn't provide for me in a more traditionally maternal way, but at this point the protector in me truly wants to wash away any guilt or anxiety she has about what she's done right or wrong when it comes to being a mother. I want us both to let that go, because I want to cherish the relationship we have now while we still have it.

Like everything in life, my relationship with my mother is a work in progress. It has gotten easier over time, but there are still moments when it's challenging or overwhelming. Basically, when it's good, it's good, and when it's bad, it's a nightmare. But I'm proud of the fact that through it all, we've remained close. And there have been instances when she did show up for me. It was imperfect care, but it was still care. Any relationship can live in a duality. Our parents can give us love, joy, and amazing memories, while also unloading a lot of their shit onto us and unleashing trauma that follows us into our adult lives. That's true no matter how privileged you grew up, or how rough you had it. It's on us to do the work, forgive those who might have hurt us, and heal, so that we can stop the cycle rather than project our shit onto our children or the other important people in our lives. Generational trauma is real, and being the person who slows it down or stops it in its tracks—that is noble work. And it's critical work on any journey of self-love.

Cindy Rigsby is a fixture in my Peloton workouts, and I try to share only the wonderful memories in my rides because a) I'm not trying to bring down the mood, and, more important, b) so many of my core memories are tied to playful or silly moments with my mother, and I want to share that joy. That's the relationship, and the woman, I want to celebrate. I've sprinkled those stories into classes throughout my Peloton career because, when it comes down to it, there is no Cody without Cindy.

Fun fact: Everyone thinks I use "boo" in my rides because it's the vernacular of gay culture. And that's not entirely false. But the true roots of "Bye, boo!" lay where all my origin stories do. With Cindy. She has been calling me Boo for as long as I can remember. As a kid, I was always Boo or Bear. That it's a part of gay lingo is fitting, but as with so much of my life, it's ultimately an ode to Cindy.

CHAPTER ELEVEN

Body-ody-ody

One of the most unexpected outcomes of working as a fitness instructor has been a vastly improved relationship with my body. As a kid, the general message that came at me from all directions was that I should look like Marky Mark in his Calvin Klein underwear. I wasn't a particularly overweight kid, but I had a belly and zero muscle definition. Over time, I learned to manipulate my physique—I could build bulk with excessive exercise, or lose weight with extremes of eating (no carb, low carb, low calorie)—but it was always sort of miserable. The window of time where I was able to say "I have this body and I really like it" was tiny. There was always something "better" than what I had. Better shoulders, better thighs, better ass.

Working at Peloton pushed me physically, and it helped me understand my own strength. I could lift heavy weights; I could do exercises at high speed. The job gave me an appreciation for my body that existed outside the fact of what it looked like. And I tried to infuse that same appreciation into my rides. My message to riders has never been *You need to look like me because I'm in great shape* or *You should work out with me so you can have a similar body.*

There are workout chains where the entire brand is about getting their clients to look a certain way. The instructors all need to conform to a body type because that's what the company is selling. But as a fitness instructor, I never lead with that. I always lead with humor because I want to bring levity to a serious and sometimes scary situation. Exercise can be intimidating, especially if you're new to it, so I focus on the storytelling and on sharing my vulnerability because people find safety and connection in those moments far more than in the way I look.

During the pandemic, Peloton exploded in popularity. At first, I was just trying to figure out how to survive in this new world like everybody else. The company had gone public five months earlier, and I had been given equity and shares, but now I was having the same fears and concerns as people across the country: What's going to happen to the economy? Am I going to lose my job? Are these assets going to be in the toilet? Are we going to go into a depression?

Luckily, Peloton established status as an essential business, which meant we could stay open and continue creating new content, which was great for me personally because it meant I could leave my house and do my job and retain some sense of normalcy, but it was also great for me professionally, because people who wanted to exercise while on lockdown were turning to Peloton classes. More people were buying bikes and discovering our content, and my classes in particular got attention, I hope because they were a bright spot of positivity in a really dark time. Suddenly Peloton was a household name. The product was showing up in TV shows, instructors were getting partnership deals, the stock prices shot up. It felt like a moment I'd been working toward and preparing for long before I knew if that moment would actually come. I had spent years figuring out my brand and the voice of my content, I had already done some small interviews and press, so when all eyes were suddenly on us, I was ready.

During that period, I was often compared in the media to Jane Fonda, which of course is incredibly flattering, but if I had to pick a fitness icon that I relate to, or even aspire to, it would be Richard Simmons. This man had wild hair and bright short-shorts and he was so over the top, so comical, that he made people feel safe. He was approachable. This was not a Billy Blanks, Tae Bo, super-cut aspirational figure. This was a larger-than-life grown-ass man in crazy costumes, and it was easy to laugh at him, but it was also easy to overlook the fact that he truly empowered people just by being his silly authentic self. He was willing to go on TV and act a fool and be flamboyant, knowing that he was creating a career for himself but also that he was helping those who felt uncomfortable in their own skin and ashamed in their own bodies. Remember *Sweatin' to the Oldies*? He filmed those videos with a group of real-life full-figured women who most likely had some insecurities about appearing in a workout video. (Who wouldn't?) But he was holding space at the head of the class. He was like, let me stand in front of you and be my weird self, and people will be so distracted and captivated by me that you will end up feeling more secure. Because if you're a plus-size person going to work out, especially in the '90s, you might be afraid that you are going to be made fun of. And here was this guy who was happy to absorb all the weird stupid energy for you in order to make you feel more comfortable.

In retrospect, I think Richard Simmons's approach was the genesis of my own philosophy on fitness, whether I knew it or not. One day when I'd been teaching for a while, I suddenly had a thought about him, no doubt something about his tiny tank tops and short-shorts and pop culture icon status, and the parallels between us became clear. He's often depicted as this comedic figure, someone to laugh *at* not *with*, but when we mock him or parody him, we overlook the fact that this man did a lot of positive things for a lot of people. He invited people into a space that was otherwise closed to them, or at least unwelcome and scary, and he made an impact.

What Richard Simmons did is exactly what I'm trying to do when I get on the bike each day. I sit on that Peloton and I dance and act a fool and share funny stories and make fun of myself, and I do it so that people will feel seen and supported and so that they'll try something that scares them. Fear, as we know, is a massive roadblock to fitness—people hesitate to try something because they think it's going to suck or it's going to be too hard or that they'll look crazy doing it. If I can be like, *Here, hold my beer, I'll look crazy for you,* they might feel safer to try something new, even if it's messy. Coming to that realization, and seeing those similarities, gave me an extra bit of permission to keep pushing the envelope and keep being as authentically myself as I can be.

Of course, Richard Simmons's reign as the king of aerobics peaked in the 1980s and '90s, a time when weight loss was the primary goal of almost any fitness routine. And, listen, I don't think there's anything inherently wrong with wanting to get more fit or lose weight or change your body.

I believe in having goals. But you have to be realistic about your expectations, and you have to be honest about the *why.* Change takes time. I know we live in an instant-gratification culture, but when you start any new routine or regimen you have to allow time for it to succeed or fail before you change trajectory or decide something isn't for you. You also have to consider that the images you see, or the people you aspire to look like, are not always realistic or within your reach. You don't have the same genetic makeup as whichever person you're holding up as inspiration. Not to mention the people whose bodies our culture historically celebrates—the JLos and Beyoncés and Jennifer Anistons and, yes, Marky Marks—their livelihood is tied up in their appearance. Looking good is literally their job, so those hours when you are in the office, they might be at the gym. Also, you don't know what kind of help they've had—liposuction, steroids, who knows what else.

Speaking of which! Let's talk about plastic surgery. There are people out there flying to foreign countries in order to get fat removed from various parts of their bodies—their stomach, thighs, lower back—so that they can inject it into their butt to make it larger. The Brazilian butt lift. It's not the safest procedure, y'all. Your body, your choice, but I'm here to tell you that squats are much easier than a BBL. You can do some lunges, do some squats, drink a protein shake—they will make you stronger and feel better about yourself, and I promise that ass will get bigger. That's my approach to cosmetic procedures in general. Live your life, but you may want to try putting in the work first. You want to get liposuction? Get liposuction! But have you tried diet and exercise? Let's give it a shot. It's hard, but it's not as invasive or scary. You want to do a cycle of steroids? Okay, but have you tried protein shakes and lifting? Maybe try those first. I'm sorry, but most BBLs look crazy. Most face-lifts look crazy. Most lip augmentations look crazy. Filler looks crazy! Less is more! I'm good. I know I come from a place of privilege, so maybe I'm off base, but a bigger butt just isn't worth the risk to me. Not to mention, when you get a BBL, you can't sit on your own ass for, like, four weeks. That's more work than squats! So maybe let's give it a good think before we go for Miss New Booty, okay?

I'd be a hypocrite to sit here and tell you not to compare yourself to someone whose body pays the bills without admitting that of course, yes, I am one of those people. I know that my body is very close to what's considered "ideal," and I know this face is pretty! But I exercise A LOT, and I think about what I'm putting into my body all the time. All the time! It's a part-time job. Plus, I work with a nutritionist, because if I want my body to operate at peak form, I need to fuel it correctly. I've become pretty regimented in what I eat, because the more I can keep my nutrition consistent the better. About 80 percent of what I put into my body is boring and disciplined—my goal is almost always to sustain my weight (not easy to do when you're teaching hours of cardio a week) or put on a bit of muscle mass while keeping my body fat low. To make that happen I have to prioritize protein, which is harder than you might think. I put collagen in my coffee, because that's thirteen grams of protein, or sometimes I just eat a pack of turkey because it's full of protein and I have to get it done. I also drink egg whites in the morning. Yes, drink. I don't have the energy to cook them. I keep a carton of MuscleEgg liquid egg whites in my fridge—they're pasteurized, I'm not trying to get sick—and throw them down the hatch first thing. Should any of you out there want to do this, consider yourself warned: They will fuck up your stomach for two or three days. Then your body gets used to it and you start pooping normally. But the minute you stop drinking egg whites daily, when you try to add them back it's like your stomach is starting over entirely. It's weird.

But like I said, my eating is 80–20. I keep my boring regimented diet during the weekdays, yet I still have three or four slices of pizza a week and I'll have a cheat day or a cheat meal on the weekends when I'm out with friends. I used to be all about sweets on cheat days—I could eat a pint of Ben & Jerry's from the bodega on the corner in one sitting—but lately I've been leaning into salty a bit more. Maybe that's a product of knowing too much about sugar, because the more I learn, the more I understand that it's so bad for you. That said, I seem to have controversial opinions when it comes to sweets. Starting with that Ben & Jerry's.

My flavor of choice, hands down, no question, is Phish Food, which I've come to learn is not for everyone. It's the marshmallow that really gets me together. I have similarly strong feelings about carrot cake. Brace yourselves: You need the nuts. This is polarizing, but I'm outing myself here and now as a nuts-in-baked-goods kinda girl. We live in a country divided on a lot of topics, and nuts in baked goods? Put it at the top of the list. You either love it or you hate it. The thing is, those of us who love it, we're more adaptive. You give me a piece of carrot cake without a nut and I'm low-key about it. It's like, "Okay, this doesn't have nuts, it would be better if it did, but I'm still going to enjoy it." The non-nut-having people are all, "This has nuts! I fucking hate it! How dare they!" The girls get so upset. Just eat the nuts and stop complaining.

So yes, while I'm a fairly disciplined eater these days, I still indulge. There's no food that's absolutely off-limits or that I would entirely refuse to eat. Except Diet Coke. That's where I draw the line. I really wish people would stop drinking it. It's a strong statement, I know—the girls love Diet Coke—but I would rather just have a regular Coke. Have one beautiful, gorgeous regular Coke! It tastes like America! Coca-Cola is the official flavor of the United States, and I'm here to call out anyone who claims Diet Coke tastes better. It doesn't. It's all chemicals. And I don't know the full science there—I barely passed chemistry— but it definitely tricks your brain into thinking you're having sugar, and that can't be good for you. Just have the Coke! I honestly don't understand it . . . you'd rather have three Diet Cokes when you could just enjoy one regular Coke? This will probably be the paragraph in this entire book that gets the most pushback, but I'm fine with that. I really do not like it.

There was a time when any book written by a fitness personality would be a weight-loss book. Back in those days, these pages would probably be called *Bye, Booze! Drop the Alcohol, Lose Weight* or *Spin Cycle: Ride Your Way to a Better Body.* I am so happy to be working in this industry at a time when the conversation has shifted toward becoming the best version of yourself and celebrating what you're capable of rather than how little space you take up. The people who ride with me aren't there because of how I look. They value me for who I am—for my charisma or humor or work ethic or compassion. And deep down, no matter how fixated we get on outward appearances, that's what we all want. We don't want to be judged on our looks. We want to be valued for what we bring to the table. That ass might be assin', but if there's not more to you than a rockin' bod, I am most definitely passin'.

XOXO, CODY:
MORE READER QUESTIONS

Q: I'm dating a guy who doesn't seem to know basic female anatomy. Is it my job to teach him?

A: In this day and age, with Google, TikTok, and Wikipedia at our fingertips, a man should be doing his own research and building his knowledge of the toys he wants to play with, i.e., your coochie. Unfortunately, even in 2023, men are fucking stupid. You've gotta decide if you want to have the awkward conversations and be his clitoral sherpa, or if you don't have the time for that and want to move on to someone who knows their way around a vagina. But! Being his sex crash-test dummy has the potential benefit of more orgasms in your life. And if he's a bad student you can always expel him.

Q: I recently "broke up" with a friend, and we share the same friend group. It's really awkward. Any advice for getting through this?

A: Everyone and everything has a season in our lives, and it's okay when that season is over. Not all our relationships are meant to last a lifetime. If you've done your best to reconcile and make the friendship work—you've had the hard conversations and taken time apart and none of that is helping the relationship function—it's time to let someone go. Think of your mutual friends as parents in a custody battle—you're going to have to share them, and it won't always be pretty. You might have to exclude yourself from some outings for a while.

Q: I have a great partner but I'm not turned on by him the way I used to be. Can we bounce back?

A: I was recently talking to an older friend, one who's had marital problems for more than five years. She and her husband both felt disconnected, and their sex life was nonexistent. Through therapy and hard conversations, they've been able to reconnect and find physical passion and love again. Sometimes our lack of physical attraction is actually resentment or mental blocks we need to work through. If this is someone you've been with for a long time, I wouldn't completely give up hope. But I *would* roll up my sleeves and do the work. If you've been dating for only a short time? Give it a few weeks, maybe a month, and if there's no coming back from the ick, let it go.

Q: I peeked and saw the ring, and it's . . . not good. Should I say something?

A: Babe, I don't understand this. You want to be surprised but don't like the surprise. If you wanted to control every aspect of your engagement then you should be the one proposing, or you and your boo should have talked about this and gone shopping for the ring together. Are these moments about expressing and celebrating love, or are they just milestones that feed your bridezilla ego?

Q: Is it possible to be in love with two people at the same time?

A: The answer is yes, but I think it's dependent on the situation. Situation number one: You are still in love with an ex-partner while falling in love with a new partner. This can leave you torn. I would advocate that you simultaneously let go of the old while taking a leap of faith into the new. Sometimes you need new love in your life before you can completely let go of the old one, so don't be afraid to love your new partner wholeheartedly—it will help you let go of the baggage of the past. Situation number two: You might be in a current relationship and start to believe you're in love with somebody else. I very much believe that most of the time when this happens, you're just distracted by the new bright shiny object, and you're confusing that fascination with love. In this scenario, I would suggest you pump the brakes. Don't give up on the thing you've already invested in for the shiny new object. Situation number three: You might be polyamorous and have the need to love multiple people at the same time, in which case you need a partner who is willing to explore that with you.

Q: What's with the Mickey tattoo?

A: First of all, contrary to popular belief, I'm not a Disney adult. There's nothing wrong with being a Disney adult, but I'm no Disney adult. Still, it's a reminder to be silly, to be a kid, and to not take life too seriously. It also helps me to remember to give my inner child the things I couldn't always get when I was a kid. When I go to the Disney parks, my tattoo is a reminder to buy the useless shit I want and eat all the sugar I want.

Q: I think my husband should always have my back, even if I'm in the wrong. Is that crazy?

A: You are absolutely wrong for wanting this, but it's also human nature to want it. A good partner will always have your back when you are in the right, but we also want partners who are going to challenge us and tell us when we're wrong. The beauty of a relationship is having someone to push you and make you want to grow. If you insist your man back you up even when you're wrong, there are going to be a lot of arguments where you make an ass of yourself, so you better be ready and willing to say you're sorry when that happens.

Q: My man still hasn't left his wife. What should I do?

A: Girl, read that question back to yourself! Do you really want to date someone who has cheated on his wife with you? And what makes you think this man is going to be different with you when he's taken no time to reflect on his decisions, no time to figure out *why* he wanted to cheat, and no time to find new ways to behave? You're just another peg on this wheel of misfortune. Love yourself enough to find a man who's single, and one who's willing to be honest. Also, bitch, stop wrecking homes.

CHAPTER TWELVE

In the Ballroom

Standing on the podium, surrounded by Jojo, Amanda, Iman, and their partners, there was no part of me that thought I might have won *Dancing with the Stars.* Jojo and Iman had gotten straight tens for both of their final dances — Amanda and I did not. Scores were only part of the equation, but still, they mattered. The bigger tell, for anyone paying close attention, was that Amanda, Jojo, and I were still wearing our final dance looks, while production had asked Iman, and only Iman, to change back into his opening performance outfit. It didn't take a rocket scientist . . .

Tyra was doing her most dramatic, suspenseful reveal voice and I tried my best to look like I was on the edge of my seat. But while it would have been lovely to win, I was content in the knowledge that it wasn't happening. All the finalists got the same money — you didn't get extra cash for winning the mirror ball trophy, so financially I'd come to the end of the *DWTS* road. Even more important, the announcement of the winner meant it was over. I'd be getting on a flight the next day, going home for good, and I was so fucking excited to be done.

Looking back, the biggest LOL of my time on *Dancing*

with the Stars was how confident I was when the idea first came up. *I can dance,* I thought. *This should be fun and easy. A tailor-made path to take me to the next professional level.* Some of that was true . . . some of it was very, very not.

But let's start at the beginning. The idea of me being on *DWTS* started floating around in April 2021. My agent, who'd seen a lot of his clients compete on the show, brought it up, and I was immediately interested. At that point, my career had changed drastically. The pandemic brought Peloton into more homes, which meant my classes had seen a huge influx of riders. And those riders liked what they saw. Suddenly, I had a much bigger profile. My social media accounts were growing, brand partnerships were coming my way, and articles were being written about me—it was exciting and overwhelming all at the same time. I used the opportunity to continue building my personal brand, because I'm always interested in seeing what's next. I'd been at Peloton for six years by then, and I had pretty much mastered teaching thirty- and forty-five-minute bike classes. That part of my career ran efficiently on far less brainpower or physical power than it did when I started. I don't want to say I was on auto drive, exactly, because that implies I was coasting or phoning it in, and that's not the case. I was still putting my heart into every class I taught (and I still do), but six years in I knew the formula that worked. I knew how much time I needed for prep, and I could rely on that knowledge to produce entertaining, challenging, and successful rides. It simply took less work to produce the same result, which allowed me more time to explore other projects.

I was also, by then, in my mid-thirties, and I am aware

that being a cycling instructor may not last forever. This kind of work is hard on the body—I could get injured at any moment. And Peloton is a company with a lot of eyes on it—their needs could change as quickly as you can say, "It's not personal, it's business." I certainly don't expect any of that to happen, but who the hell knows? Nothing is guaranteed in life, and when it comes to earning a living, I like to have a backup plan, and a backup to my backup. Seizing the opportunities that came from my newfound visibility felt like a no-brainer, especially the opportunities that would allow to me flex my existing muscles while also building some new ones. My approach to expanding my career and my brand is pretty straightforward: As long as I'm having fun and there's purpose behind it, I want to try new things.

And there was another reason I was interested in *Dancing with the Stars.* It's something we don't always talk about, though I don't know why the fuck not, if we're trying to be real with each other. As Peloton got more popular and my career grew, I was seeing more financial success. Not just from my salary, which obviously had grown since I started at the company, but also through opportunities like branded social content and other partnerships or appearances. New opportunities meant new income streams, and you can be damn sure I wanted to maximize my bank account. I know what it feels like to struggle, and—spoiler!—it's more fun to live comfortably. Once you attain a certain level of financial security, you want to maintain that. I've got mortgages to pay and a lifestyle that I enjoy living, and I worked hard to attain that lifestyle. So yes, I want the opportunities to keep coming, and sometimes the only way of ensuring that happens is to be strategic. Which is why when my agent asked if I'd consider joining the cast of *DWTS,* it was an easy yes. Here was a massive platform that could introduce me to a new audience and let me try my hand at live prime-time television. Plus, it paid. Fuck yes, I wanted to give it a go.

Our first meeting with ABC was with casting. Rob Mills, a top executive with ABC's unscripted department, was in the meeting, and only after the fact did I learn that his being there was a big deal. "He doesn't usually get on *Dancing with the Stars* calls," my agent said. *Okay, fierce.* It always feels good to be courted. And it did feel like we were dating—I was pitching myself to the show, casting was pitching the show to me. That was in May. But then, silence. I went the whole summer without hearing another word about it. I figured my casting was dead in the water, which was a bummer, but then, on a Sunday about a month before the season thirty premiere, I got a call: *Did I want to officially be in the ballroom?*

The minute I agreed to join the cast, all that cool confidence I'd had about this easy path up the career ladder started to fade away. I went from *It's going to be a massive audience!* to *Holy shit, it's going to be a massive audience.* I had full-on anxiety attacks about it. One morning, only a couple of weeks before we started rehearsals, I found myself second-guessing the whole thing. Was I sure I wanted to do this? It was going to be a lot of fucking work, and I didn't really know what I was doing. I was used to judging reality TV contestants from the comfort of my living room couch. Was I ready to be the one getting judged? I also knew that whatever nerves I was having in that moment—in my bed, in New York, weeks before the premiere—would only get worse. I was pretty spoiled at that point. I no longer got nervous stepping in front of the Peloton camera. It was easy and came naturally. But here was something brand-new, with high stakes, that wasn't completely comfortable. Of course I would get nervous. And this wasn't just pedaling in front of a camera, either. I would be dancing!

Despite having been a professional dancer, or maybe *because* I'd been a professional dancer, I was terrified. I knew enough about dance to know how easy it is to fuck up a step and throw a whole number off. It's really hard to get back on beat once you've bungled a routine. Back when I was dancing for a living, I did a club gig for Kat Graham, who was on *The Vampire Diaries* at the time and trying to kick off her singing career. I missed a step during the routine and I could not, for the life of me, get back to it. I kept fumbling and falling, and it was so embarrassing. With *DWTS*, I knew the opportunities to botch a routine were huge. And I wasn't wrong. The nerves never did go away. Every time you go live on that show it's a massive adrenaline rush, and you must conquer fear and anxiety, while hitting every step, in a ninety-second dance. It's fucking terrifying.

I started traveling to L.A. for rehearsals a few weeks before the season started. Because of my work at Peloton, I'd decided to do the show in a sort of vagabond way, flying back and forth every week between New York and L.A. I had to wear a hat and sunglasses and keep my head down each time I traveled because the show told me to hide my face from the paparazzi until the cast was revealed. That was probably the most celebrity-esque thing I've ever had to do, which was exciting, I guess, but also weird. Honestly, fame is bizarre. I get stopped nearly every day at this point—it's either "You're Cody from Peloton" or "You're that Peloton guy from TikTok!"

Peloton instructor fame is a very approachable kind of fame. I'm not Brad Pitt. Most people aren't going to walk up to Brad Pitt if they see him on the street, but people feel they have access to me. I'm not labeling that as good or bad; it is what it is—people feel connected to Peloton instructors' stories and our lives and our success. Some members have been with us since the company's beginning, so they feel like that neighbor who's watched you grow from a baby in diapers to an adult heading off to college. Other members are newer, but they're dedicated riders who spend thirty minutes with you every day. They've listened to your stories about middle school or your mom or your favorite singers, and they've been responding to you in their heads, from their homes, for ages. When the opportunity to talk IRL comes up, they can't help but jump on it. It's endearing and of course I'm grateful for it, but it's definitely weird how people assume they know you. Of course, I would never normally disguise myself in public—whenever I'm approached by Peloton members I stop to chat or take a selfie. I know what a privilege it is to be in that position. Still, watching people do a double take or take surreptitious pictures of you as you're going about your daily life . . . it's strange.

My first trip to L.A. was to meet Cheryl Burke and record the big partner reveal. At that point, I didn't know who else was in the cast. I'd heard some rumors about a couple of people, but the whole thing was very cloak-and-dagger.

Until then, it had been an ignorance-is-bliss situation—
I could comfort my nerves when I got too anxious by pretending what I'd signed up for wasn't *that* big a deal. But on
the afternoon of my arrival, I spotted my first cast member,
and that delusion was quickly put to rest.

I'd been whisked to the rehearsal space straight from
LAX. The plan, the producers said, was for me to enter the
studio, react to the big reveal, and start rehearsing. But I was
no dummy. I knew this was going to be on film. It was supposed to seem casual, but come on. I had just gotten off a
six-hour flight, and I looked it. I was not trying to show up
for my first recorded moment of prime-time TV looking
busted, so I convinced the producers to let me go to the
bathroom to freshen up. When I knocked on the door, a
female voice with a British accent responded: "One minute!" The next thing I knew, the door flew open and this
incredibly fit brunette walked out. She was wearing a mask
so it took me a minute, but then it hit me: OH MY GOD,
THAT IS SPORTY SPICE. Mel C.! I was so gagged. Star-
struck. I honestly didn't know how to react. I was, am, always will be a die-hard Spice Girls fan. I have watched *Spice
World* more times than I can count—I can recite the entire
movie verbatim. Realizing that I was about to compete on
the same stage as this icon was completely surreal.

The only other cast member I'd heard about at that point
was JoJo Siwa. The news had leaked that she was going to
compete, and I was psyched. JoJo is so fierce! She built an
entire brand when she was just a kid, and the fact that she
could come out and still have all this shit on lock is so im-
pressive. That she was doing a same-sex partnership was especially killer.

I learned the identities of the other cast members about twelve hours before the rest of the world did. We had a big cast reveal on *Good Morning America*, which took place at Disneyland in the wee hours of the morning, so we did a Zoom call beforehand to meet for the first time, or at least to get a glimpse of one another. But being there at Disneyland, with these other celebrity contestants and Robin Roberts and Lara Spencer, felt like a wake-up call. Most of these people were famous-famous, whereas I was more niche and internet famous. My cast had not only a Spice Girl but NBA player Iman Shumpert, *Beverly Hills 90210* actor Brian Austin Green, *The Office* star Melora Hardin, and Olympic gold medalist Suni Lee. They were people who'd had long careers in the public eye or world-famous accomplishments. Imposter syndrome started to show its busted-ass face. *What am I doing here?* was a refrain that ran often through my head.

The first of those *What am I doing here?* moments came during the *GMA* reveal itself. I hadn't told my stylist exactly where I was going because I thought I wasn't allowed to—I'd signed all kinds of confidentiality docs—and I didn't do a great job communicating the type of appearance I was trying to dress for. The outfit we decided on was very athleisure: a light green sweatshirt, black joggers, and white sneakers. I get that I'm a fitness instructor, but it wasn't the best choice. I felt like the small-town girl who'd just gotten off the bus. My *GMA* segment was with *Real Housewife* Kenya Moore, influencer Olivia Jade, and *Cobra Kai* actor Martin Kove. Kenya and Olivia both wore dresses and heels, and Martin wore a black velvet blazer. They were dressed for a night on the town; I was dressed for the gym.

I should have leaned into my personal style and rocked something cuter. Fashion is something I care about, it's an extension of who I am, and I don't feel like my full self showed up that morning. But sometimes you make mistakes. In that moment, I got the message loud and clear: *Bitch, it's time to step it up.*

Until then, I was just kind of winging it . . . with my clothes, but also with my *GMA* appearance in general. This was one of my first appearances on a major national outlet, and I usually put a lot of pressure on myself to make the most out of small opportunities. I'm always trying to make a moment punchy, but I wasn't thrilled with the segment. It was fine, but I didn't seem as comfortable and clever as I would have liked. It was clear I was entering the big leagues, and I needed to get with the program.

I did have one advantage coming into the competition, and that was my fan base. Throughout the entire show, I felt extremely supported by my Peloton colleagues and the members who ride with me—it felt like I had a team behind me going into this scary new adventure. The Peloton community is an unusually engaged audience. They weren't just rooting for me; they were rooting for the community as a whole. Their dedication to Peloton was palpable, and they wanted to show up. That's not something an actor from an old TV show or a musician—even an incredibly talented musician—necessarily has. Sure, they have fans, but their voter base is not as organized or as mobilized. (You know this bitch is not running for office—oooh, the dirt they'd dig up—so this is as close as I'm gonna get.)

It never really occurred to me, when I signed up for *DWTS*, to take a break from teaching Peloton classes. That probably would have been the sane thing to do—I should examine my workaholic tendencies—but I also don't know if I would have had the same experience if I'd canceled my rides for three months. Taking my rides in real-time, while I was competing, was exciting for members. My competition experience was part of my class content—I told stories, commented on dances—and it rallied voters. It was the right choice for me and my success on the show, but it was also really fucking tiring.

Despite how hard I've worked in my life, I do not subscribe to hustle culture. I don't love glorifying endless work or bragging about being burnt out. Take a vacation! Enjoy your life! That said, my *DWTS* schedule, especially before I got sick with COVID, was insane. I would do rehearsals and Peloton classes in New York during the week, then I would fly to L.A., usually on Saturday, so that I could be in the ballroom on Sunday for camera blocking, a rehearsal in the TV studio for the production crew to see the dance and figure out when to cut to what camera or when to shoot confetti in the air. I'd stay in L.A. through the show on Monday night, and when it was over I'd take the red-eye from LAX to JFK and get home at six in the morning. I'd get about four hours of sleep on the plane and then start the whole thing over again.

There were a lot of exciting moments, starting with seeing Tyra Banks in person. She is a pop culture icon, and I was totally gagged when she knew my name. I was walking through the set and she looked at me and said, "Hi, Cody Rigsby!"—full name—and I was like "Oooooh, okay! Fierce!" The fans of that show are not nice to her for some reason. I don't know why they don't like her. She's Tyra! I really do not get it.

Getting to know the rest of the cast, at the beginning and over the course of the season, was also a pleasure. Amanda Kloots and I had some really touching conversations about my experience being raised without a father around. She was curious about my upbringing and naturally had a lot of questions as she was trying to navigate that space after having lost her husband. Christine Chiu, of *Bling Empire*, gave everyone a bottle of Ace of Spades champagne (with an engraved case!) because she's rich as fuck. It's still sitting on the bar cart in my apartment. She was very into *DWTS*— a self-professed superfan. As happy as I was about the exposure and fun and challenge of the show, I was also excited about the paychecks. Christine probably didn't even fill out the direct deposit form! Country singer Jimmie Allen was a good guy, too. I got along with him really well. I have so much respect for him—I love his story and what he's doing with country music. And Mel C. and I had some lovely conversations, but we didn't become friends exactly. I didn't want to bog her down with my crazy energy, and I never really got over the fact that I was standing in the ballroom with a literal Spice Girl. But across the board, everyone was cool, and getting to know them was a highlight of the experience.

The season premiere went off without a hitch. Training was hard—we worked with our partners, who were also our choreographers, anywhere from four to eight hours a day, Monday through Saturday, and then we ran through the number another three times during camera blocking—and dancing live on national TV was scary, but everything went according to plan. And then, week two . . . Cheryl got COVID. She couldn't appear in person in the ballroom, and since I'd been closely training with her for weeks, neither could I. We were scored based on a taped rehearsal earlier in the week, and luckily made it through. But then, a week later, I tested positive. It was so disappointing. We'd worked so hard, and it had already become clear to me that this experience, while valuable, was going to kick my ass. This hiccup bumped it up from difficult to nearly impossible.

The week I was sick, if you can believe it, was Britney week. What. The. Fuck. Obviously I love Britney—loving Britney was my brand before I even had a brand—and I was devastated that I wouldn't have my moment to fuck shit up in the ballroom. And Cheryl had requested stripper poles. Fucking stripper poles! And this go 'round, since Cheryl and I were both home sick, they couldn't even air a taped rehearsal. Instead, production came up with a plan: We would dance "together" remotely, each from our own home.

It SUCKED. Not the dance, per se—we did our best with it—but that whole COVID moment was rough. I thought very seriously about quitting the show that week. I was just . . . done. I'd been full of anxiety from the moment the season started, but this situation pushed it through the roof. It was not the way I wanted to show up on national television. I am someone who always wants to excel and do my best and look my best, and this felt like a budget version of what I had to offer. Physically I felt okay—I've had COVID a few times, and this was the easiest and chillest of them all—but I still wanted to lie on my couch in the fetal position and not do anything. It was so defeating—a definite low point. I was sick, I was run-down from all the traveling, I was disappointed that I had to put on this low-rent *DWTS* showing, and all the pressure from fans and judges was fucking with my head. I'd only been on two episodes so far, and I already couldn't believe how much work it all was. But then my boss from Peloton, Jen Cotter, called me. "Sure, you can quit," she said, "but I think you can get through this. Maybe once you get past this week it will be smoother sailing."

Cheryl was even more straightforward. "You are not quitting; we will figure this out," she said. "Don't fucking go there."

In the end, I got myself out of my slump. I knew that if I quit I'd be giving up an opportunity that would help me grow. *Nah, girl, this ain't your time,* I told myself. *Get up, figure it out, keep pumpin'. You got this. You are going to figure it out like you always do.* One thing I always try to remind myself, especially in hard times, is that I always figure it out. Every challenge, every misstep. I've always made my way through.

The best advice I've ever gotten was from my friend Miles Redd. In a moment when shit got especially hard, he told me: "No matter what you're scared of, just show up—you'll figure it out." That's the motto I live by. Just show up. When faced with a fight-or-flight moment, we have three options: We can quit, we can stick it out while freaking out, or we can relax and breathe and trust ourselves. Options two and three will get you the same outcome, but option three causes much less damage. Feeling stressed and anxious will wreak havoc on your brain and your nervous system, making the journey entirely unpleasant. Breathing through the moment and trusting that you'll get where you need to be—it doesn't make the work easier, but it makes the experience tolerable, and perhaps even enjoyable. *Get your ass up, show up, get it done.*

I'm so glad I decided not to quit. From that moment forward, I tried my best to show up from a place of calm and trust rather than a place of anxiety. And thank God, because that remote broadcast situation was out of control. I couldn't go outside with COVID, so I had to clear all the furniture out of my living room and find space for it in other parts of my apartment. (My place is big for a New York condo, but it's definitely not a-spare-room-for-all-your-living-room-furniture big.) Production shipped me black boxes that looked like they held the nuclear codes. I guess they were for sound and internet and . . . I don't even know what else. My home looked completely chaotic—wires, screens, speakers. It was crazy. And then I had to trust that everything I set up would work. It was live! I was dancing in my living room and I had set everything up myself to broadcast on national television. There were endless opportunities to fuck it up, and not in a good way. Cheryl and I tried to work the virtual thing to our advantage, or at least come up with as many gags as we could to make it interesting—we passed something from my screen to hers, that sort of thing—and some of it read and some of it didn't. In the end we just had to fight, and we both fought hard.

Our scores from the judges were shit—they didn't exactly go easy on us given our situation—but we made it through. Like a cat with nine lives, we lived to dance another night.

As it turned out, getting COVID might have been a

blessing. (To be clear, we were both vaccinated, and neither of us got very sick.) It was a unique story line, and it incentivized Peloton to help me find a better approach to the rest of the season than flying back and forth across the country every week. We ended up creating a makeshift studio in an L.A. showroom so I could teach from the West Coast. They weren't the best-quality classes, but they did the trick.

My *DWTS* experience was indeed smoother sailing from there, but it was never easy. Staying put in L.A. relieved a lot of travel stress, but every week on that show is a different challenge. You're learning a new dance, or two new dances, for every episode, so even if you were good at the last one you might be shit at this one. There's pressure from fans and from the audience at home, and from the judges. And look, it's a TV show, so it's not all as straightforward as it seems. Certain weeks, I got frustrated with the low scores the judges gave me. But my fans voted early and voted a lot, so the judges could score me harshly without knocking me out of the competition. I had to learn not to take it personally. At the end of the day, it's a television show, and my fans kept me from bottoming out. That voter turnout (there's my political run again) really helped.

Still, as great as the fans were, there were times when I couldn't help but get on Twitter and read my critiques. I'd scroll through nasty DMs, reviewing the many ways in which the trolls thought I bit it. That shit is hard! For some reason, it really affected me during Janet Jackson week, which was the episode before the semifinals. There were fewer contestants left, so I guess it's logical that the noise would be louder—there was a smaller pool of people for the haters to come for. I had to tap into my positive self-talk: *You are fabulous, but not everyone is going to like you. That's okay. You opened yourself up to this and you can't let anyone's opinion get you down.* Easier said than done, but it was helpful nonetheless.

Throughout all the many challenges, one of the most encouraging and frankly eye-opening moments came courtesy of—who else?—Melanie Jayne Chisholm, otherwise known as Mel C. (Full name for the real ones.) She was leaving rehearsal as I was going in, so we were chatting in the parking lot, sort of hiding behind a car because the paparazzi were there taking pictures. (See previous note on the weirdness of fame.) I was telling her how nervous I was, how stressful I thought the whole situation was, and she was like, "I know, I'm freaking out. This whole show makes me so anxious." Mel. C herself admitted that she, like all of us, didn't know going into it what being a contestant would entail. Here was this pop culture icon who has sold out massive stadiums and performed in front of giant crowds and literal royalty and headlined a movie, but she felt the same pressure as I did— she wanted to be good and she didn't want to look a fool and she was super nervous. She was so generous with her honesty in that conversation. It was a really human moment. Here's someone I've looked up to my entire life, and she was feeling the same way I was and riding the same emotional roller coaster. It was an "I see you" moment, and it was really grounding. I had this realization of *You are not the weakest link, you are not horrible, you're having these feelings because you are human and humans get nervous and excited and scared.* If Sporty Spice herself still had anxiety around performing, then I sure as hell shouldn't beat myself up for being nervous throughout this crazy adventure. We were all doing the best that we could, and that's all you can ever do.

For a massive television production, there were plenty of human moments like that behind the scenes. My relationship with Cheryl, above all, was a reminder to me that we're all just people. Cheryl has been on *DWTS* since its second season. She knows how the show works and has experience with all types of partners, but she was challenging to work with at first. She was hard on me, and it always felt like there was something else going on with her. She could have been trying to prove that she was a hard-ass dance instructor, but it felt like there was more to it. During the week leading up to Queen night, we were getting ready to perform the foxtrot. It was a challenging dance, and she was frustrated that I wasn't picking up on it more quickly. All week, Cheryl was unusually tough on me. Very emotional and cutthroat and sometimes downright rude. I had to be up-front and address it. "I don't know who you worked with before or what your working relationship with them looked like," I said. "But you can't speak to me that way. There's just no way you can talk to me like that, so please figure your shit out." Being confronted like that made her even more upset, and it was a challenging rehearsal that culminated in a big argument.

We got through it, and over time I came to realize that Cheryl was under a huge amount of pressure, probably even more than the rest of us. At that point, she had been on the show for twenty-six seasons. Twenty-six! Being on the show for one season, I got a taste of how taxing it can be. There's the physical component of learning a new dance (or two) every week and having to do it with a person you barely know. There are the constant critiques from the judges on the things you are doing wrong, not to mention the media attention and criticism from the press and social media. Because Cheryl had been doing the show for decades, the media was always especially interested in her, and people on social were especially tough on her. You can have the world's thickest skin, but at some point that level of scrutiny will affect a person. Then there was the body image part of it—people were always coming for Cheryl for being too skinny or too thick. As a man, I didn't have to deal with that at all, and Cheryl had faced it pretty much every week for twenty-six seasons. I can't imagine. Plus, she got sober a few years before we started working together, which is a journey she's been honest and vocal about. If she once used alcohol as a coping mechanism and crutch to help her deal with the pressure of *DWTS* and numb the pain, she was now sitting in that difficulty and working through it on her own. That is hard work! In the moments when it seemed she was not coming from a place of kindness, I tried to remind myself of that. It was a lot to deal with for both of us and there was probably more baggage in our rehearsals than there should have been, but that's what you get when you place two big personalities in the same space and put a challenge in front of them.

I had a lot of love for Cheryl by the end of our run together, and I still do. The process was a good reminder that in any partnership you need to meet people where they are, and you often can't take their behavior personally. A person's actions are almost always more about them than they are about anyone else. When we behave poorly, it's tempting to make up a story that it's someone else's fault—that they aren't acting right or working hard enough—but it's usually about what *we* are going through, not anything the other person is doing.

Around the time our season was ending, Cheryl finally opened up to me about the other stuff going on in her life, the deeper stuff I'd been sensing in our hardest rehearsals. "This season has been fun and a great distraction, but now I need to figure out if I want to be with my husband," she said. That's some major shit! She was dealing with heavy baggage that had nothing to do with me, and of course some of that stress spilled over into the rehearsal studio. One thing I know for sure is that even when you want someone to calm down or behave better, you can't make it happen. They have to get there by themselves. Cheryl is talented, she is strong, she is resilient. I truly cannot fathom doing this show for more than two decades! It takes a physical and mental toll on a person, and you have to be strong-willed to get through it. But there was nothing I could say to get Cheryl to see in herself all that I could see. She had to come to it on her own.

In time, she did. I reached out to Cheryl recently to give her kudos, because even from her social media presence I can sense an energy shift. There's more confidence and joy there, and I'm so happy for her. I'm sure that leaving a marriage is terrifying, but I'm happy that she figured out what was best for her.

Despite any challenges Cheryl and I may have had, our partnership worked. We got third place! My favorite dance of the whole season was the paso doble we did on Janet Jackson night, which was right before the semifinals. We slayed. It was honestly the only dance I had fun with. Not that I didn't enjoy any of the others, but I wouldn't describe them as fun. That week, in which I did both a paso doble and a cha-cha, I was just like, *Fuck it. I want to have fun and dance and be stupid and silly—this is fucking Janet Jackson!* By that week I had let go of the anxiety. I'd reached the goals I'd set for myself, making it through seven weeks and elevating my personal platform and earning some good money. As much fun as I had that night I remember thinking, *Honestly, HONESTLY, if I go home tonight, I'm okay with that. It's totally fine! Please?*

We didn't go home, and as much as I slayed that dance, I butchered the Argentine tango in the semifinals. I felt bad. It's Cheryl's favorite dance, and I started the whole routine about a count early. We'd already done one dance that didn't go especially well, so when it was time for the tango, I was shaking like crazy. If you look back at the video of that performance, you can see it: me, on a podium, holding my very unsteady arms up like a bullfighter before the dance starts. I was the most nervous I'd been the whole season, and my mind was racing—*holy fuck holy fuck holy fuck.* I guess I was so eager to get it over with that I dove in a beat too soon. The judges didn't call me out for it. Props to Cheryl, she knew where she was in the music so at some point I step-step-lifted her up and I heard her whisper a very stern "Don't move!" in my ear. We held a long pause and got back on the count but it was terrifying. We got okay scores and I didn't think we'd make it through, so I was shocked when I ended up in the final four.

The finale was gravy. I didn't expect to be there, so I wasn't nervous. I tried hard to have fun with it, because I'm usually so bad at enjoying things in the moment. I knew this was a once-in-a-lifetime experience, and I wanted to be present for it. And I loved my finale dance. I wore a sequined jumpsuit and danced to Todrick Hall—I was in my element. The true Cody finally showed up on screen. We got all tens and it was just a good-ass time.

Iman Shumpert won the mirror ball. He's a cool guy, he had some great dances, and I was happy for him. And I was thrilled to have placed third. *Dancing with the Stars* was one of the two hardest things I've ever done in my life. (The other was a weeklong silent retreat that I'll tell you about later.) Between rehearsals and shows and my Peloton teaching, I did not have a single day off between Labor Day and Thanksgiving of that year. Making it to the finale and placing third was a powerful reminder of my own strength. There are so many things in life that can bring us down, scare us, or make us doubt our self-worth or abilities. Throughout that whole season, especially in the most difficult moments, I stayed rooted in my work ethic, my hustle, my skills, and my community. After all that pushing—through some really fucking low moments and hard moments and scary moments—the reward wasn't the money or the notoriety, but the reminder that I am pretty damn resilient.

CHAPTER THIRTEEN

Lost and Found

If the perils of addiction were simmering under the surface of my childhood, then as an adult they became a blazing fire, courtesy of my best friend Oscar.

We met in 2010 or 2011—it's hard to pinpoint the date because I can barely remember a time when Oscar wasn't around. I was at a bar with my friend Cory, and I while I can't recall much, I can tell you the evening ended with Oscar and me making out in the back of a taxi. But that was a onetime thing. While the two of us became incredibly close, we were never involved romantically.

After that first meeting, Oscar and I spent more and more time together. We'd go to brunch on Sundays and drink bottomless mimosas at a restaurant where I was dating the bartender; we'd grab dollar pizza slices for lunch and end up spending the entire day together. Oscar loved to dance—we'd stay up late into the night disrespecting people's sons at clubs across New York. We traveled together, too. My first-ever international trip was with Oscar and some other friends to Israel for Tel Aviv Pride. He was always down for adventure and seeing new places. He was more into being a tourist than any of our other friends, so we would explore foreign cities together, finding the best food or shops or places to meet local men. (When it comes to foreign languages, I generally know enough to order food and get laid. That's all you need, you heard it here first.) He was also one of the last friends I did adult sleep-overs with—we'd make it a point to hang out all day and then one of us would crash at the other's place. When I was homeless for two months after Dylan burned my clothes, I crashed at his apartment for a few weeks. We went through a lot of life's ups and downs together, and we did a lot of growing up together.

Oscar's birthday was a day after mine. Quintin's is June 7, mine is June 8, and Oscar's was June 9. None of us were big birthday people—we didn't like all the attention—so we always shared our celebration to diffuse the weird birthday energy. Yet somehow I never knew how old Oscar actually was. He was an interior designer, and because he wanted to be taken seriously in the design world, he always lied about his age. He'd add a few years to seem more established, be-cause people like to hire designers with more experience under their belt. I was always confused about which birth-day he was celebrating—it was impossible to keep track of what age he'd told which friend group. *I don't know how old Oscar is,* I'd inevitably tell an inquiring birthday guest. *You're going to have to ask him.*

As close as Oscar and I were, I could always tell there were some demons lurking in the shadows. Like so many young professionals in New York City, Oscar used pre-scribed Adderall to get work done. He would procrastinate until the last minute and then stay up for a day and a half straight doing nonstop work. He was finishing school while freelance designing—taking on way too much, especially for someone with horrible time management. "I took an Adderall and ordered this extreme-ass coffee," he'd tell me (sometimes it would be a Red Eye energy drink), and I'd be like, "What the fuck do you need all this caffeine for? Ain't no way I could deal with that." I sensed that he had an addictive personality. Whatever he was doing, he would do in excess.

For a while, that addictive behavior seemed to zero in on party drugs. I don't refrain from having my fun, and I've had plenty of mornings where I've woken up on the hot mess express, but a bitch can tell when shit is getting out of hand. Over time, Oscar's drug habit veered into problem territory. He would get fucked up to the point that he was basically asleep at the clubs when we were out at night. One night I had to literally carry him out of a bar because he was completely passed out. When that happens once it's like, *Okay, girl, let's think about our decisions.* Twice, it's frustrating. But when it's the third or fourth time, it starts to get worrisome, because now there's a pattern of behavior. I wanted to help, and I was concerned, so I confronted him. It happened time and again, and I tried everything: I told him I was worried, I tried to get him to acknowledge the problem, I gave him ultimatums. I even told him if he didn't stop I'd involve his mother, whose approval was incredibly important to him, because I simply didn't know what options I had left. I wanted so bad to help.

For a long time, this behavior continued. Watching someone you love self-destruct is terribly painful, and eventually I had to create some boundaries. I couldn't control Oscar's actions or make his choices for him. He had to want to help himself, and for a while he simply didn't seem to care. Separating the person from the disease became difficult. I knew Oscar heard my pleas, and yet he carried on with the drugs anyway. It's hard not to take that personally, especially when you've begged and threatened and opened up about your fears. Creating boundaries in those situations is its own challenge—you have to navigate this constant dance of wanting to help the other person but also wanting to protect yourself. Oscar and I never stopped being friends, but after I repeatedly tried and failed to get him to acknowledge his problem, I kept my distance for a while. He would always be important to me, but I stopped assuming his struggles as my own, because I knew that I had done all I could. I could control only myself, so I had to try to protect my own sanity and health. In this case, that meant not trying to save someone who wouldn't try to save himself.

Eventually, it seemed like Oscar was getting a handle on things. I was proud of him. He didn't appear to be doing any more drugs, and while he was not totally sober—he was still drinking—he appeared to be a lot better. And maybe he was, at least temporarily. The drinking seemed like nothing serious. Casual, social drinking, as one does. Alcohol had never been a problem for Oscar, so we weren't worried. But when a bunch of us got together for Friendsgiving in 2019, it was clear there was more to the story. I watched Oscar pour whiskey into a highball glass, with no ice, no chaser. He filled that very tall glass halfway and took it down quickly, and then had another. It was not your average casual drink at a holiday gathering—even at a wild holiday gathering. Andrés and I both clocked it. *Something is not right here.*

Despite having been through some tough conversations, Oscar and I were still important to each other. Yes, I'd taken a firm stance on what I could and could not be around, which might have put a strain on our once-easy friendship, but we had a long history together. I loved him. He'd been my best friend for nearly a decade, and while we were no longer spending every weekend together, we talked regularly. On February 23, 2020, we touched base via text:

> *Me:* Hey
> *Oscar:* Hey girl, I'm not feeling well, let me text you later.
> *Me:* Ok, no problem.
> *Oscar:* I took myself to the ER.
> *Me:* I hope you feel better. Wait, what? Do you need help?
> *Oscar:* No, I'm ok. Stomach just hurt too bad.
> *Me:* Ok baby, let a bitch know.
> *Oscar:* I'll keep you posted.

Those were the last words I ever received from Oscar. *I'll keep you posted.* I wrote back a few hours later to check in and got no response.

It turned out that Oscar had taken his drinking to an extreme, and either nobody knew or only a few people knew, and I was not one of them. At that point in late February, he'd been drinking so much that his kidneys had started to fail, and the doctors put him under soon after he arrived at the hospital. He was on all these machines, and Steven, his boyfriend at the time and a doctor, was constantly interpreting what was going on. Some days the news felt encouraging—*He needs a kidney transplant but he's going to be ok; it will be hard but he'll make it*—but then the next day it would switch to *Things aren't looking good.* Another day later: *It's getting better, there's a possibility he'll come out of this.* It was a roller coaster. Oscar was on life support for a few days (which felt like a few months), but ultimately he lost his battle with alcoholism.

Oscar's death was the hardest loss I've ever faced. This wasn't like losing my dad, some mythical figure I'd never met. This was a friend I knew intimately. He was flawed, but that's because he was human. He was my best friend and a wonderful man, and losing him was devastating. I've spent a lot of time processing my grief, but also my guilt, over his passing. I put up boundaries to show him how worried and pained I was by his behavior—how worried all of us who loved him were—and, more important, to try to force *him* to take it seriously. But there are days I wonder if I was too hard on him. If that firm stance put such a strain on us that he couldn't let me in.

Loving someone who's battling addiction is so hard. You want to show up unconditionally, but when they continue to make dangerous or toxic or unhealthy decisions, you have to protect yourself. It can feel like a catch-22—you know you need to create boundaries, but by creating those boundaries you feel like you're abandoning someone you love. I tried to help Oscar in every way I knew how, but eventually I had to take some distance to protect my own mental health. Still, even if you know, intellectually, that you can't save someone who doesn't want to be saved, it can be hard to shake the doubt.

The December before he passed, Oscar and I had a long conversation about what I was going through with my mom. This was at the height of her struggles in New Jersey, just after she'd had lithium poisoning. I was fairly quiet and secretive about it at the time—maybe because I didn't want to embarrass her, maybe because I was in denial—but I told Oscar. I was so overwhelmed, I said. I was taking care of my mother in this new capacity (Oscar always made fun of me for using the word *capacity*), and it was much harder and much more complicated than I'd expected. I told him about how I had to clean her up from a bathroom accident and how I found her naked in her bed. It was traumatizing, I said, and I didn't know if I could handle it. We had this long talk where I opened up, not because I wanted him to do anything or come up with a solution but because I needed a friend. I needed emotional support, and for someone to ac-knowledge that I was going through it. I needed to be heard.

Not only did Oscar hear me, but what he did next was one of the sweetest things anyone has ever done for me. I should start by noting that I am never surprised by any-thing. I can always tell when someone is asking a question with the intention of surprising me or trying to sneak some-thing by me. I always see it coming. But after this specific conversation, I had to go away for a couple of days for work. When I got home, Oscar had painted my bedroom and installed new light fixtures and put up art. He literally took his talents as an interior designer and gave them to me as a gift by redecorating my room. This man knew I was hurting, and he showed up in this very personal way to make me feel loved and special. I was so incredibly touched.

Of course I wish I'd been able to help Oscar. I wish I could have saved him. I ended up sharing his story on *Dancing with the Stars,* because for Queen night, Cheryl and I did our foxtrot to "You're My Best Friend." It was a hard week for us—it was the same week that we got into our only real fight, and I'm sure my stress levels during rehearsals weren't helped by the knowledge that I was telling this personal story on national television. Out of respect, I asked Oscar's mother for her permission to share his story, and that was a tricky conversation. Tensions were high for everyone. But it was really important to me to share queer stories on *DWTS.* I wanted to celebrate this amazing man and our wonderful friendship, but I also wanted to be honest about what had happened, in case it might help someone watching.

Addiction issues and drug abuse affect the queer community in a really harsh way. LGBTQ adults are almost twice as likely to suffer from substance abuse disorders than straight adults, and I think for a lot of gay men, during those younger years when our straight friends were exploring their sexuality or experimenting with drugs, we were hiding in the closet trying to keep it all together. When you repress that experimental energy for so long, it can eventually explode. A lot of gay men come out, move to bigger cities where they will feel more accepted, and become like kids in a candy shop—finally able to explore their new world and maybe leaning a little too hard in that direction. There are, of course, a ton of reasons why someone might turn to drugs or alcohol, but addiction is prevalent in the gay community and it's something that people don't talk about enough.

Despite whatever qualms Cheryl and I had with each other during Queen week, she supported my sharing Oscar's story. She's a recovering alcoholic, and sharing our personal experiences with addiction helped us connect and understand each other. "Sometimes, when we're under huge amounts of stress, we give in to the worst parts of ourselves," Cheryl told me. The way she said it—that collective *we*—compelled me to look inward. I don't struggle with substance abuse, but I know that I've used sexual behavior to cope with feelings of discomfort. I've cheated on boyfriends, I've made bad dating decisions, I've gone back to people I know aren't good for me. Those decisions have usually aligned with times in my life when everything else felt hard. Destructive coping mechanisms are difficult to shake even for those of us with no addictive tendencies.

Coming to terms with addiction and its constant presence in my life has been a hard-earned education in patience, grace, forgiveness, and control. Sometimes the universe—or God or whatever/whoever you think is pulling the strings—puts the same challenge in front of you, over and over, until you've learned the intended lesson. So much of healing comes from forgiveness—forgiving ourselves and forgiving the other person for keeping their secrets or making mistakes. Anger is a natural part of the grieving process, but remembering the person you lost for all the reasons you loved them, rather than all the reasons you're still mad, is a much lighter lift.

It's easier said than done, I know. I have cycled through anger toward my father, toward my mother, toward Oscar, and toward myself. For so much of my life, the only constant was instability, which is probably why I usually try to conquer fear through control. If I can be in charge, then I won't be disappointed or hurt, right? But there's no hiding from pain. Losing Oscar taught me that once and for all. We can't control anything in life, so we have to love from a place of abundance. Love as if you don't know how long that person will be around, because you don't. Love them for who they are and all the reasons they make you smile, even if their actions cause you pain. We cannot control anyone but ourselves. We can't control the outcomes of other people's struggles. But we can control how hard we love those people. How generously we love them. When all is said and done, knowing that we loved with grace and compassion and a full heart will be what helps us heal. In the wreckage of all that is lost, that's what's waiting to be found.

THINGS THAT MAKE ME
FEEL RICH

Ordering something for the table at a group dinner. But just know, if you order appetizers, restaurants love to scam you by plating them in odd numbers so groups can't share. So then you'll have to order two for the table! Which makes me feel even more rich, because yes, I *will* order two.

Having a refrigerator in the garage. You have so many beverages that they need their own fridge, *and* your family can afford to buy large quantities of meat, as if you've just won *Supermarket Sweep*.

Paying extra for guac. Yes, I know it's extra.

Drinking water out of a large green glass bottle. There's something about the risk of chipping my tooth that feels like living on the expensive edge.

Wearing new white sneakers in the rain.

Bringing an empty suitcase to buy clothes on a trip. Not only are you paying to check the extra luggage; you're spending it twice so you can go spend *more* money. You're ready to buy anything, and you don't have to stress about getting it home.

Choosing multiple beverages at brunch—water, coffee, a mimosa, and a green juice for detox, because you're hungover from last night.

Keeping your own log-in—and not sharing any—for streaming services.

Allowing your iPhone to rawdog it, no case in sight. Some of y'all are leaning into AppleCare a little too hard.

CHAPTER FOURTEEN

I Don't Want to Be Friends

I've had six serious boyfriends since the age of seventeen. I've said "I love you" to five of them. I've actually loved three of them. (The other two . . . well, I meant it when I said it, but looking back now I know better.) Two of them caused me immense amounts of heartbreak.

Breakups suck. I wish I could say they get easier over time, but I'm not here to lie to you. Instead, I'll say that every breakup is hard in its own way, and every breakup has its own lessons to teach us. And also that sometimes you don't want to learn a hard lesson, you just want to be a petty bitch and make your ex jealous, and that's okay, too. I'm in no position to judge. But for the purposes of your romantic education and enlightenment, I'm going to tell you about my own history of heartbreak, the lessons I've learned along the way, and the rules I've come up with as a result.

A quick note before we start: The first rule of breakups is that there are no rules—we think stupid shit and do stupid shit when our hearts are broken, so adhering to a guidebook is not always the priority. Still, if you keep these truths in mind, you can at least start the healing process. And if you can't focus on these truths just yet, if all you can do is get under someone to get over them . . . well, I'm not above that, either. Don't get me wrong, it won't help you heal, but it'll feel good for a night.

Before I came out of the closet, my only real experience with breakups was what I saw on TV and what my friends went through. My girlfriend Kacie had many more relationships than I did in high school—she was straight, I was gay and closeted—and, in retrospect, I wasn't an especially supportive friend when the fellas did her dirty. I didn't give great advice, and I wasn't a good listener or shoulder to cry on because I hadn't been through it myself. My wise counsel went something like: "Get over it! It's just a guy!" I was super eye-rolly about heartbreak—these girls and their drama!—which is an easy place to be until you find yourself on the receiving end of an "It's not you, it's me," elbow deep in Phish Food, and watching *The Notebook* again. (My breakup movie of choice is actually *Closer,* with Clive Owen and Julia Roberts. It shows all the fucked-up parts of relationships, heartache, and getting back together. I find it so cathartic. But I sometimes just watch *Spice World*. Comfort food.)

The first time a relationship sent me to the couch to cry and eat my feelings was after my breakup with my first real boyfriend, Connor. (My very, very first boyfriend was Nolan, the cheerleader I met at the mall and dated for a summer. But you've heard about him already, and our breakup was not especially newsworthy. The big takeaway there was that I'm definitely into guys.) Connor and I met at Bravo, a small Italian restaurant chain in North Carolina where we were both waiters. We dated for more than a year and then broke up over the summer before my senior year of college. He was a year older, so he was graduating and moving to New York, and we both knew that long-distance wasn't going to work. Still, I was heartbroken. It was the first time I'd experienced that specific type of pain. It was so different from anything I'd felt before, and I just didn't have the tools to process it. And so I did what all the girls do. I listened to Danity Kane's *Welcome to the Dollhouse* and was all up in my feelings about songs like "Poetry." It was fucking dramatic.

I can look back now with a healthy dose of perspective, but oh boy, I saw nothing funny about my predicament back then. It felt raw and shocking and painful. But it was necessary. Before you can figure out how to learn or grow from a breakup, you need to feel the feelings. A breakup is a loss, and the grieving is real. There's no way around the pain; you just have to go through it. And so I did.

As is often the case, especially in college, what eventually helped me get over Connor was meeting the next guy: Zane. We started seeing each other my senior year—he was a few years younger—and we dated long-distance after I moved to New York. He joined me in the city a year later, and I was excited to take on New York with a partner by my side. I felt like a capital-A Adult.

Zane and I stayed together for about nine months in New York, which is not to say that things were hunky-dory for that entire stretch. Sometimes there's a moment in a relationship, and it can happen long before the actual breakup, when you know there is no future. With Zane, this happened around the time I booked my first Victoria's Secret Fashion Show, dancing for Katy Perry. We were in the middle of a fight when I got the call saying I'd landed the gig.

This was a career-defining moment for me, and no matter what we were arguing over (I can't even remember), I wanted to celebrate with the person I loved. But Zane couldn't, or wouldn't, set aside his anger in order to congratulate me. I'd been working toward this moment for two years, and the fact that this man couldn't press pause on the fight to acknowledge this major milestone? In that moment, I knew the relationship was going nowhere. I remember thinking, *Oh wow, you can't drop this bullshit to hype me up? You gotta go.*

More time passed before Zane and I broke up. Ultimately, our ending was mutual. And no, that's not just me pretending I wasn't dumped. I know it can be hard to believe a breakup was truly mutual, but in this case we both recognized the relationship was a mess. Nothing was adding up, we were young, and we were growing in different directions. We both knew it was time to move on, although that didn't make it any less sad or painful. Still, it was a good education in knowing when to call it quits, because I should have trusted my gut the minute I realized the relationship had no future. A partner who can't root for your success, who can't set aside his own baggage to cheer you on in your brightest moments, that is not someone who deserves to stick around.

Next was Michael. My breakup with Michael was the first time that the decision to end things was entirely my own. It was not mutual, not even semi-mutual. Despite the fact that he had a husband, Michael wanted to stick it out. That man had a lot of unprocessed trauma. He was working through a lot of shit. Actually, he *should* have been working through a lot of shit. Instead, that shit festered and manifested as behaviors that either hurt me or pushed me away, over and over again. It was a toxic, wild relationship, with so much fighting that I hit a point where enough was enough. I couldn't do it anymore. *Sorry, boo, time's up.* Michael tried to make things right and talk me out of leaving and win me back, but the more he tried to convince me that I was making the wrong decision, the more certain I was that I was doing the right thing.

Eight years after that breakup, it's still impossible for me to say definitively when it's time to cut the cord with someone. But when you know, you know. If a relationship isn't serving you, if it's not making you feel loved and supported, if you don't feel like you can be raw and vulnerable with the person sharing your bed, it's probably time to say goodbye. That seems like as good a rule of thumb as any. Also, don't ignore red flags. Sometimes there are A LOT. (For my gays, whenever anyone says they are a total top it annoys the fuck out of me and makes me skeptical; for my girls, anyone who doesn't eat pussy. What is that?) Still, we put blinders on. Love is a powerful drug—it's far too easy to fall under the influence.

This doesn't mean you should throw in the towel the minute things get hard. Deep and meaningful relationships don't come around that often. If you're in one, it's probably worth fighting for. And I'm not talking figuratively. I don't trust couples who don't fight. It makes no sense to me. If you never fight, then you probably don't care! So, no, don't let a relationship go the moment it doesn't bring you joy. But if you've tried to do the work—you've listened to feedback, let go of resentment, looked internally, and endeavored to change—and it still doesn't feel right, you might have to accept the truth and make a break. There's power in letting go of someone, or something, that doesn't serve you anymore.

While Michael and I were dating, I met Matheus. There I was, standing in the gym locker room, when this very hot Latin man approached and gave me his number. I had to tell him, a bit begrudgingly, that I had a boyfriend. But I saw him at parties a lot, and once Michael and I broke up, Matheus and I started going home together from time to time. We hooked up plenty, but it was relatively innocent— nothing penetrative. Of all the boyfriends I've ever had, Matheus is the one I dated the longest before having sex. Even after we started officially dating, it was another month or six weeks before we did it. I'm not usually a proponent of waiting—I'm more of the *Do it and do it now!* mindset— but in this case the buildup felt oddly special.

Matheus and I dated for two years, from 2014 to 2016. It was my first truly adult relationship—I was in love, and I felt loved. We shared common interests and laughed at all the same jokes. He seamlessly fit into my group of friends. The sex was incredible. I started taking Portuguese lessons because he was Brazilian and I wanted to meet his family. It was one of those deep connections where you can just feel that something special is happening. The real deal. And as a result, my mind started wandering toward the future. For the first time in my life, I was envisioning my life with someone.

There was only one problem. Right around the time Matheus and I met, I'd come to the realization that maybe monogamy wasn't for me. I had, in one way or another, cheated on every boyfriend I'd ever had. It's not something

I'm particularly proud of, but it's what happened. By the time I'd been with Matheus for four or five months, I knew that I cared deeply about him and that I wanted to be with him. I didn't want to hurt this man, and I definitely didn't want to cheat on him, so I figured I should be open and honest and communicate my feelings. I was still learning a lot about relationships, but I knew enough to know I didn't want to fuck up a good thing.

It was not an easy conversation. Matheus wanted a partner, he wanted monogamy, and he didn't want either of us to be sexual with anyone outside of the relationship. We had one of those long talks, the desperate kind where you both want different things but you also want each other. Hours later, it was clear we were at an impasse. It was also clear that we loved each other a lot, so we came up with a solution that is so obviously flawed in hindsight that it makes me cringe just to put it on the page. Our path forward? *Let's put a pin in this and keep going.* Because ignoring a problem always helps it go away.

You probably know where this story is going. The following summer I was planning to travel with friends, so Matheus and I decided to revisit the monogamy conversation. This time we came up with some rules. I couldn't tell you what they were anymore, but I can absolutely tell you that I broke them, which meant I cheated, which was the opposite of what I wanted to happen. I gave in to the parts of myself that can be egotistical and selfish, and I pushed the limits.

Eventually, I told Matheus what happened. I am a horrible liar, and I hate keeping secrets. Consider how much I share with thousands of strangers in any given Peloton ride.

I'm an open book! So you can imagine how transparent I am with the people I love. I want honest conversation in every relationship—romantic, professional, whatever—and in this case, even if I wanted to hold it in I wouldn't have been able to. So I owned up to my mistakes, and Matheus was, predictably and deservedly, devastated. And yet! We were in love, so we decided to keep trying.

It's a beautiful thing to romantically love another person. It's one of the best feelings in the world. To crack yourself open and be vulnerable and love wholeheartedly, it's euphoric and brave and exciting and profound. But love is not enough to make a relationship work. I wish it were. We've been sold that dream by every Disney movie, every romantic comedy, and it's just not real. Love is the foundation for a lasting partnership, but you need compatibility. You don't have to see eye to eye on every single thing, but my therapist says a good rule of thumb is 80–20. If you're compatible on only 80 percent, and there's 20 percent where you aren't, maybe it will still work. But once you get into that 75–25 range . . . that 25 percent can really fuck things up.

As it turns out, consensus on monogamy is pretty huge on the compatibility scale. Five months after I took that vacation where I broke the rules, I went on another one. I thought Matheus and I had healed, and I didn't cheat this time, but I guess the fear that I might flipped a switch for Matheus. The day I got home, I had barely set down my luggage before he uttered those dreaded four words: "We need to talk."

I was heartbroken when Matheus ended things. I'd never been through that kind of breakup before—not sleeping, not eating, powerless to get off the couch yet totally unable to relax. It was brutal. I was deeply in love with Matheus, and I had fooled myself into believing we'd resolved our issues. It's amazing to reflect on that relationship now, because the ending seems so obvious and inevitable. I want to scream at myself, *You don't want the same things! This will never work! Anyone could have seen this coming!* But back then? I was in a bottomless pit of despair, and I felt immense shame for hurting this person I cared so much about. The pain was, frankly, shocking. It's easy to blame the other person for a breakup and play the victim, but I was under no illusions. I had to work through some shit. I had to change.

Whenever I'm going through a hard time and someone says, "You'll learn from this," I want to smack them upside the head. Still, when we continually put ourselves in situations that don't align with who we are, the universe has a way of making us do the work. The Matheus debacle forced me to start asking some hard questions of myself: *Why do I feel like this? Why do I think my needs and desires are more important than protecting someone I love?* I didn't sit around blaming Matheus; I tried to take accountability and responsibility. It wasn't easy. But as a result of that pain and heartbreak—or as a way to wade through it—I was inspired to start meditating. I started therapy. Those two pathways unlocked so much for me: They taught me how to process uncomfortable feelings. They gave me an outlet to talk about what's going on in my head instead of keeping those thoughts inside or redirecting them into actions I'm not proud of. I'm so grateful for the tools that came from that breakup. I wanted to understand why I made the choices that I did, and in the end I unpacked a lot of childhood trauma and began to understand a lot of the challenges I've covered in this book.

People say time heals all wounds. I fucking hate that expression, especially when it comes to breakups. Time doesn't heal shit. You don't sit there and let the clock run out and suddenly feel great. It's what you do with that time. You grieve, you allow yourself to cry and vent and feel the feelings, you take responsibility for the things you might have done wrong while not beating yourself up for your mistakes. These are the skills you need in order to heal from a breakup. From there, it's one step forward, two steps back, and the journey is filled with all sorts of emotion and bad decisions along the way.

If what I learned from the Matheus breakup was to take accountability and process, with Andrés, my next boyfriend, surviving the breakup was about living in the gray area. When a relationship ends, it's easy to villainize the other person or villainize ourselves. With Matheus, I took on the bad-guy role. He was right, I was wrong. But the reality usually lies somewhere in the middle. When Andrés and I broke up, it wasn't "You fucked *this* up" or "I did *that* wrong"—nobody cheated on the other, there was nothing black or white I could point to as The Problem. I had to recognize where I fell short, but I also had to be sure I didn't romanticize Andrés or vilify him either. Not an easy feat in the throes of heartbreak.

When Andrés and I first met, my life looked completely different from the way it does today. We started dating in 2018. During the next year and a half, my personal life took a few big hits. First, I moved my mom to New Jersey, took over her medical care, and had to confront a much grimmer picture of her health than I'd ever anticipated. I also lost Oscar, which obviously caused a lot of grief and emotional turmoil. Then, eighteen months into our romance, a global pandemic hit. Andrés and I were stuck at home, spending every day together. That sort of forced togetherness is hard for any relationship—when you're still relatively new to each other, it can be a real shock.

Meanwhile, during COVID, my professional success began to skyrocket. I was taking on projects and responsibilities that I wasn't entirely prepared for and hadn't been given the tools to deal with. The stock price of Peloton shot up and I was able to sell some of my shares, which meant I had a cash flow I never could have imagined—a blessing, obviously—but learning to manage that newfound money was like exploring a foreign land. I was also trying to navigate being a (fairly) public figure. I wanted to capitalize on my success while keeping the machine running and the opportunities coming. In addition to all of this, I was trying to have a personal life that involved a partner and his feelings and his life. I didn't always get it right.

Andrés and I argued a lot in those days. Like many couples, we seemed to have the same fight over and over. Then we'd make up or decide to move on, but without any actual tools for resolution, we'd end up back in the same place in no time. During one especially heated argument in May 2022, I asked if we could go to couples therapy. "We have a great connection and I love you," I said, "but without some help we're going to keep having this same fight."

"I don't know," he said. "I think I just need some space. We'll be fine, but I need a minute."

It made me anxious, but I trusted him when he told me that we would indeed be okay.

Three days later, Andrés came over to watch *Drag Race*. We weren't fighting, but there was a tense and awkward energy swirling, until, seemingly out of nowhere, he burst out: "I can't do this anymore."

Andrés said he'd been feeling hurt and pushed away by me as my career had changed, and I was devastated. I'd tried to be the best person and partner I could be, but I was also determined to capitalize on my success while I could. When fame or notoriety come quickly, you have to consider the idea that your fifteen minutes might run out. It's irresponsible not to. I certainly don't intend to be a flash in the pan—I'm working my ass off to protect against it—but, especially when it all first started, I thought I'd be dumb not to do everything I could to make the most of every opportunity. Still, what I learned as things ended with Andrés is that success and money and a thriving career is not everything. I was so focused on those things that I neglected myself and my relationships. The people in your life have to be number one—when relationships get lost amid the drive and ambition, it's really fucking lonely.

When Andrés broke it off, it would have been easy for me to get defensive or say he didn't understand. That he wasn't supporting me. But I tried, again, to take responsibility for my actions. My behavior, and even more so my communication, was not my best. It was not in alignment with my intentions. But this time I also cut myself a little slack.

My life had changed drastically in a short amount of time, and there was a learning curve. I was dealing with a lot, and I only knew what I knew.

There was one other variable that threw a wrench into my breakup with Andrés: Our relationship was public. At least more public than any of my other romances. I talked about Andrés in my rides. I posted pics of us together on my Instagram. I spoke about him at length in a *Dancing with the Stars* video package. Over the course of four years, Andrés and I built a relationship and a life that I was excited about, so I made no effort to hide it. I have no regrets about that, but the public interest was a complicating factor in getting over each other that I hadn't ever experienced.

When you live your life in the public eye, people feel entitled to real-time updates about your life. I know of what I speak, because I was one of those people. You think I wasn't scrolling for daily updates on #FreeBritney? You think I wasn't out here refreshing my feed, waiting for Shawn Mendes and Camila Cabello to announce their demise? (Not to say I told you so, but I fucking told you so.) I know there's an entire school of thought that says, *You put your entire relationship on social media—now we the people deserve to know if you broke up.* But luckily, those people aren't in my relationship. There were only two of us whose opinions truly mattered, and announcing my breakup is very much not my style. I hate cringeworthy posts that beg for sympathy from the general public. Breakups are personal! Involving other people in your drama is not cute. That is between you and your former boo.

Still, people were speculating. Andrés disappeared from my Instagram stories. Even more telling, for those who cared to dig deep enough (and those people are out there): We stopped following each other. After a breakup, you must unfollow or block your ex on social media. At least while you're trying to get over them. It's not about being vindictive or petty (though there's a place for that, too), but you can't process your emotions if your former partner's content is showing up in your feed. Watching their posts, tracking what videos they like, noting who they're following . . . it can all be really toxic. You were so in love with this person; they were so integrated into your life—it's easy to get obsessive about what's keeping them busy without you. You have to create boundaries for your own sanity. It's not permanent (you can always unblock or refollow), but it *is* an act of self-love, because you're protecting yourself from constantly getting hurt by the social media of it all.

And listen, I'm not all talk. I take my own advice. In one of my last conversations with Andrés while we were going through our breakup, I was very clear: "Hey, I might block you. I might unfollow you. It's not me trying to be a dick, it's not me trying to get you. But I can't be seeing what you're up to; it just hurts too much." I told him the same thing about having any real-life in-person contact. I didn't want to see him, at least not in the immediate aftermath of the breakup. I needed to create space and time away in order to heal.

To quote Lady Gaga, "I don't wanna be friends." That is probably my number one rule for breakups. We have to grieve relationships. We have to let them die and bury them. We have to let the hard feelings go, because there will be hard feelings no matter what. We also have to free ourselves from our romanticized version of this person, and all the fantasies we had about our future together. Because if you're ever going to be friends again, or have any chance of rekindling the romance, it has to be on a new foundation. You have to come together as new people meeting each other in your new lives. That can only happen if you've separated properly and taken time and space.

When people go directly from being lovers to being friends, it does not compute for me. The math is not mathing. There's this saying I always think of—I don't know who said it first, but the gist is that if you can go right to being friends, you're either still in love or you never were. As far as I can tell, when one person says, "Let's stay friends," it's either because the dumper is trying to soften the blow, or the dumpee is hoping to get back together. Both are dangerous! Don't do it!

But before you can cut off contact entirely, there will be a meeting, post-breakup, where you have a big talk and try to get closure and get in a good cry. You are also, in that moment, going to give that person back their belongings—all the stuff you left at each other's homes over the course of many, many sleepovers and lazy days canoodling in the bedroom. In advance of this meeting, I want you to go through the house, find as much as you can, and put it in a bag. When you see each other, return it, calmly and maturely. Now, listen good: Inevitably, there will be a moment when you find something of this person's that you missed. You'll find a T-shirt that was in the laundry, a toothbrush in the bathroom, a fucking Christmas ornament you bought together that you stored in the basement. Do not hold on to it! Nobody needs whatever crap they've been living without for months. If you start to collect another pile of Tom's socks or Pete's books, you're just trying to find an excuse to reach out. You want to have another interaction and yes, I'm calling you out. Let it go. They don't need their hoodie; I promise you they already bought a new one. It's all good. Throw it in the goddamn trash.

After that final meeting, it's goodbye, adios, sayonara. Do not text this person, do not DM him, do not drunk dial his ass after a night out at the club. However. No matter how hard you try to keep your distance, you will probably run into each other at some point over the course of the coming months. It's bound to happen, especially if you've spent the last year, give or take, frequenting the same restaurants or hitting up the same bars. When this happens, some guidelines to keep in mind:

1. You have to say hi. You must. Even if you're so incredibly mad at this person, even if you never want to see him again or want to scream at him for hurting you or punch him in the goddamn face, you cannot be the girl who ignores and you cannot be the girl that makes a scene. Say "Hi, how are you?" and then move on.

2. If you're with someone hot and in the presence of your ex, this is the moment to feel cute about yourself. Show him what he's missing! As Beyoncé said, "I'm just as petty as you are." So give 'em a show, baby! Give 'em a show! But don't make it too obvious. Be petty but tasteful. You want to leave some room for doubt. You want to be able to say, out loud and with credibility, that "I'm just doing me." You'll know you're being

petty, but the only person you should tell is your best friend. Your bestie will celebrate your victory, but don't let the general public know. Keep your intentions to yourself and maintain the upper hand.

3. I can tell you not to do it (don't do it!), but at some point you're probably going to end up having sex with your ex. There is something about sex with an ex that feels really great. There's chemistry, pent-up lust, and the validation of knowing that at some level they still want you. I can't say I haven't done it. It's a real power trip. But just know that at some point you're going to have to deal with the consequences. I've been in that boat so many times. *Don't do this,* I say to myself. *You are going to regret this!* But it feels so good in the moment. So good! All I can say is, every action has a consequence. And the consequences here will probably translate to pain.

4. If you run into your ex's friends, but not your ex himself, the rules are different. In this case, do not ask about your ex. I don't care how much you want to know what they've been up to. Don't ask! Do not try to pull a casual "How's Pete doing?" or "Tell Tom I say hi." That shit is so transparent! You are digging for intel and it's not a good look, and this person already has his allegiance. Not only will you not get any info, but the friend will absolutely report it back to your ex. No one should wield that much power. Say hello and keep it moving.

Breakups are a lot. They are complicated and exhausting and sad and painful. They can be petty as fuck and inspire stupid decisions or unreasonable behavior, and not a single one of us can claim to be immune to the grief and the chaos. The neurological and physical pain that ensues is not in your head—it's straight science, and it sucks. The only thing I know for sure, however, is that this too shall pass. It's going to be uncomfortable for some time—and I can't tell you how long it will take—but you will make it through. As long as you are processing and dealing in a healthy way, you will come out on the other end a stronger person—one who hopefully knows what you need and how to ask for it the next time around.

Andrés and I were broken up for six months. I followed all the advice I've given you here—we kept our distance, we didn't talk, we worked on ourselves, we accepted that the relationship was over. I spent a lot of those six months getting adjusted to this new phase of my career and getting my priorities straight. I figured out how to navigate my professional life without going at the hyperspeed I felt I had to in those early days of the pandemic, and built a career foundation that was strong enough that passing on one opportunity wouldn't mean the whole house would come crumbling down. One day, around Thanksgiving, Andrés called me. He wanted to meet up, and to discuss the possibility of getting back together. I'd accepted by that point that it was time to let him go, but I still loved him and cared about him and missed him. I wanted to give it a shot.

When we reconnected, Andrés and I were both new people. We had done the work individually to mend some of what was broken in our relationship, but when we came back together, we committed to breaking the patterns that we fell into the last time around. That meant going to couples therapy, and working together to form a stronger, more compassionate bond. That's not always easy, especially after you've been apart for six months. Things happen in those months, and now not only did we have to deal with our past as a couple, but we had to be okay with any relationships or hookups or behavior that took place while we weren't together.

The best advice I got in this regard was actually from P!nk, on the night of her album release party for *Trustfall*. She invited me to host the party, and at some point during the evening I mentioned to her that my boyfriend and I had broken up and now we were back together. I knew she went through something similar with her husband—they were separated for a little over a year before getting back together—so I asked if she had any advice. What she told me really stuck with me: "Whatever happened in that time apart, let it go, forgive it, and don't give it any weight." It was powerful advice, and really helped me release some resentment and anger I was holding on to. She's an amazing artist and an amazing woman, and words of wisdom from a person like that have meaning. To hear her address the very thing that had been on my mind, it helped remind me that I had to focus on moving forward rather than living in the past. That's why Andrés and I got back together in the first place, because we want a future together. I can't tell you that this is the fairytale ending, it's just where we are at this point. Will it be forever? Time will tell. For now, I want to be present in the moment, and give space for us to keep choosing each other.

CHAPTER FIFTEEN

The Fee Is Going Up

It's no secret by now that financial stability is important to me. Growing up poor—welfare poor, food stamps poor, homeless poor—leaves its mark on a person. I live in fear that any money I've made will evaporate into a puff of smoke, but through my success at Peloton I've finally been able to shift my focus. Instead of scrambling for survival, I can think about creating wealth, and that in turn has created security and stability. It's easy to say that money can't buy happiness, but whoever said that never slept on the floor of a motel for twelve months. They never juggled three separate shift jobs at one time just to pay the rent. Money may not buy happiness, but it can certainly buy peace.

Here's a tip: Capitalism ain't going nowhere. For too long, talking about money—especially talking about wanting more of it—has been taboo. But whoever created that stigma was probably the same asshole who said money can't buy happiness—and whoever first said *that* was probably a rich old white man that didn't want to share. *Tell those fools that money won't make them happy, then maybe they won't come for mine!* My personal motto is different: If it isn't making me richer or thicker, it's time to go. If my ass or my bank account isn't getting fatter, thank you but no. I'm trying to collect as much coin as possible. This is just how the world works; I didn't make the rules. Money creates opportunity—to have joy, to have stability, to have more opportunity. So get your bag. Get your bag! Because no one is going to get it for you.

It's fine, of course, if you don't want the bag. If you're happy with your life, congratulations. Fantastic. I love to see it. If you're following your passion and that's working for you, more power to you. I tried doing that with dance, and I'm grateful that I did, but at the end of the day it didn't offer stability. So I'm writing this chapter to give you permission to follow the money. Raise your fee. It's not greed; it's America. Many of the joys in this life cost a pretty penny, so there's no shame in going after the paycheck. Grab every opportunity in front of you because there will always be someone behind you who wants it just as bad or even more.

That's the approach I take with every financial opportunity that comes my way. If I don't grab it, someone else will. Take social media. We have gotten to a place in our culture where Instagram and TikTok accounts have clout, and that clout can be monetarily beneficial. If I can make an income from that, I'm going to. I don't know how long brands are going to want to pay me to hawk their products, so I'll do it until they tell me to stop. At the end of the day, having financial security will offset any shame or guilt I might feel for doing business on my social accounts. I felt plenty of guilt and shame as a poor kid, so I'd rather dry my tears in therapy with dollar bills than Kleenex.

All of this is to say: Know what you want, go after it, and have no shame. Don't be average, be savage. However! How you go about getting what you want? Your actions? That is different. Don't be screwing over your best friend or your business partner or the Uber Eats delivery guy and saying Cody Rigsby sent you. No, ma'am. I do not condone stepping on other people on your way to the top. If you're mean or nasty or using others to get ahead, that's where I draw the line. I've always believed there's room at the top; there is enough opportunity for all of us to thrive. It doesn't have to be me versus you. Not a single project I've done has been a completely solo endeavor—in any given Peloton class, there are producers and sound engineers and camera operators working behind the scenes. On *Dancing with the Stars,* it wasn't just me and Cheryl—there were PAs and costume designers and hair and makeup. When I speak at an event, there are bookers and coordinators who help make it happen. Success is never created in a vacuum, so I try to operate with a sense of compassion and gratitude for everyone who has their hand in the work that makes me successful. It's a collaborative process, and I never forget that.

In fact, in a world where we're told not to talk about money, I'm here to tell you that we need to talk about it *more.* We need to be open about how much we're making or what we're charging. Not because we want to brag but because we want to lift up the people around us. You should know how much your peers make, and you should tell your peers how much you make. If you're truly worried that sharing your salary with a colleague will take away from your provisions, then you need to level up. That's on you. Also, there is no pay equity without transparency—if we want to be sure that women, people of color, the LGBTQ community, people with disabilities, are all getting paid fairly, we need to be open about salaries or hourly rates or however it is you get that check. There's power in numbers.

Still, even in an equitable pay environment, not everyone will make the same bank. Someone with more experience, or who brings in more business, may make more than you. That's fine. Once you have a sense of what they're getting paid, you can begin to understand where you are on the spectrum. Knowing where you stand can help you set goals, or it can signal that it's time to find a new gig. In either case, knowledge is power.

When I first started hearing from brands who wanted to work with me on social, I immediately called Ally Love. "You've done this before," I said. "What's the going rate? Can you teach me what you know?" She was a few steps ahead of me when it came to branded content, and I knew she had plenty of knowledge to impart. I wasn't jealous of her, I admired her. I wanted to learn, so I asked for help.

Ally was generous with both time and information. She sat me down in the basement of the Twenty-third Street studio, where the instructors would collect in a makeshift lounge outside the green room, and whipped out her phone. "Let's take a look at your account," she said. "Your posts look pretty good, but you need more strategy around when you post. There are optimal times of day to publish content, and you want to nail the cadence so you aren't posting too much or too little. You also need to be sure you're using the right hashtags." Ally spent forty minutes walking me through her social strategy like a social media fairy god-mother, and I took her insight seriously (even though hashtags are irrelevant now). One of my biggest pet peeves is when people ask for advice and then don't do shit with it.

Know the value of someone's expertise. If you're asking someone how much they're making or how to better your business or how to get ahead in your career, and you don't put action behind the information they share, don't go back to that person again. It's an insult to their time and their energy.

The only thing I didn't do after Ally imparted her knowledge? Charge her same rates. Ally had experience. She had already proven that she could convert followers to consumers. But I absolutely latched on to her numbers as a "maybe one day." It's good to have goals, but you have to sacrifice a dollar amount when you're in a foundational space. You have to prove that you can do whatever it is you want to get paid for. Taking the lower rate now will provide the experience necessary to ask for more the next time around. And that's exactly what I did. I took the partnerships and created the content and happily accepted whatever paycheck came my way. Over time I learned to make my posts more genuine. I used humor, I pushed the boundary with content that was somewhat inappropriate, just like I do in my classes. I stopped feeling like I should post just to post. I moved into a space of authenticity, and the money followed. I learned to make good content, the clients got what they paid for, and everybody won. Sometimes you've got to play the long game.

It is, of course, a delicate balance. Whenever you start any new endeavor, there's a window during which you have to prove your worth, and that can sometimes mean working for free. When I was a dancer, I volunteered for performances so I could work with certain choreographers or gain experience in front of important audiences. That kind of sacrifice can absolutely help you get your foot in the door. But you can only do it for so long. At some point you've got to start asking the tough questions. *I've been doing the extra work, are you going to pay me more? Are you going to give me a promotion?* If yes, great. If no, okay, then I need to dial it back because I no longer work for free, or for a reduced price.

One of these make-or-break moments happened for me in my dance career around the time I started working for Peloton. I wasn't pursuing dance with the same singular focus I had been, but I hadn't closed off the dream entirely. For the right opportunity, I was still showing up, so when a friend called and asked me to come in for a last-minute audition for JLo, it was an easy yes. I hung up the phone, grabbed my stuff, and flew from Harlem to Pearl Studios in Midtown, where I auditioned alongside some other dancers. After an hour or so, the choreographer said, "Okay, you're good, now we're going to go to Alvin Ailey." I hadn't yet been told outright that I was in, but the implication was that I had gotten the job.

When I showed up at Alvin Ailey, the director and choreographer for the performance was Frank Gatson Jr., someone I'd auditioned for many times. Frank is the creative director for JLo, but also for Beyoncé and Rihanna, so yes, he's a big deal. But he's also notorious for playing games with dancers. This man is so full of himself. He loves to hold huge auditions and sit there on his soapbox and hear himself speak about how hard he had it and how you have to fight to make it in this business. He's not wrong about that, but the hourlong diatribes are a bit much, as is the fact that he is constantly putting down dancers who are busting their asses to work with him.

When I arrived at Alvin Ailey, I got right to it, learning choreography and formations—I thought I was in a rehearsal. JLo was sitting right in front of me, eating her arugula salad with salmon, and it felt like Frank was playing some sort of game with me. He hadn't explicitly said "You have the job," but he was using my labor and my energy to create the performance. I spent eight or nine hours dancing for him that day, so when he eventually dismissed us and said, "Come back tomorrow at nine A.M.," I wanted to get my paperwork locked in.

"Can you contact my agent so I can get my contract set?" I asked Frank.

"What?" he said. "Oh no. Tomorrow is going to be another audition."

I'd been in the dance world for years at this point—I knew the difference between an audition and a rehearsal, and what I had just experienced was a rehearsal. No audition I'd ever been on was like this. This man was using my free labor.

Cody, you are at a new job, I said to myself. *You can't play games with that opportunity. You can't hold on to this "maybe" anymore.*

"You know what? I'm good," I told Frank. "I don't think I'll be coming back." Sure, I would have loved to say I danced for JLo, but I had to choose myself and my future. A part of me had some nagging questions: Why wouldn't they commit to me? Was I not good enough? I was doubting my own self-worth, but I was looking for validation from people who literally did not care about me. Finally it hit me: JLo is great, but I need to worry about myself.

That was the last dance audition I ever went on.

Talking openly about money is not only about sharing salaries or pay structures. I've had a crash course in finance over the past couple of years—mortgages, equity, stock options, all of it—so when people I care about ask me about money, I tell them what I know. Why would I withhold information that could make my friends rich? The fact that your friend is going to make more money should have no bearing on your ability to succeed and provide for yourself. It just means you'll both be able to afford the lavish vacation, and to that I say fuck yes. The bougier, the better. (Speaking of money and vacations, you know what's a burden on both? Kids. They are expensive! So here's some unsolicited advice: Get your checks up before you get your cheeks clapped and make a baby.)

The truth is, I'm still on my financial crash course. Money is so fucking complicated, and as much as losing it all would be my childhood nightmare realized, I take strange comfort in knowing that I've already been through the worst. I've already scrambled for food money; I've already slept on couches. I did it and I lived to tell the tale. Might I be making monetary decisions now that will bite me in the ass later? Absolutely. But I always go back to the knowledge that I've figured out everything else in life, so I'll figure this out, too. If the market crashes, if I lose all my properties, if my investments tank, I'll figure it the fuck out. It might not be the same life, but I'll adjust as I always do, and that gives me some peace. Yes, money is the ultimate security blanket, but I also get security from my resilience, from my work ethic, and from my ability to problem solve. If it all goes up in smoke and I need to get back in the McDonald's drive-thru? *That's one Big Mac and fries, coming right up.* I'll be the fiercest girl in the window, taking orders without skipping a beat. I did it before and I'll do it again.

When you've come from nothing, or have no experience with money management, it's easy to assume you're going to fuck it up. I am constantly flooded with imposter syndrome. When I'm standing on a red carpet and P!nk approaches with a compliment? When I'm interviewing Trixie Mattel or JC Chasez or Carly Rae Jepsen during my very own talk show on wheels? When I land a fucking book deal?! There's always a part of me that worries I'll be found out—that someone will realize I'm just a kid from North Carolina who doesn't know what he's doing. But one thing I've learned over the course of my career is that most of the "experts" making the big decisions don't know a goddamn thing about what they're doing either. They were just in the right place at the right time. That's most of success: being in the right place at the right time with enough skills to safely land on the next stepping stone.

I felt that most acutely three or four years into my work at Peloton. That's when the company first gave instructors equity in the company. I was in a meeting with my boss when I got my equity grant, and seeing those numbers laid out—numbers that could be life-changing if the company did well, numbers that could help me provide for myself *and* my mom—made me cry some very happy tears. It felt like winning the lottery. Yes, I had worked hard and was an asset to the company, but at the end of the day I was in the right place at the right time to get the job interview in the first place. They say success is a combination of hard work and luck, and I don't take that for granted.

Around that same time, I got my first bonus at Peloton. In those days, instructor bonuses were based on who got the most views, and I kind of scammed the system by subbing for any ride that needed one. My individual classes didn't get as many views as those of more popular instructors, but I taught so much that it added up. At the end of the year, I had the second-most views of any instructor—not because I was the best at teaching but because I was the best at finagling the system. I got a fat bonus that year, and I used it to pay off my credit card debt. It was a thrilling moment—I'd been carrying that debt around for ten years—but there was still that little voice, murmuring in the background. "You didn't really earn this," it said. "You worked the system. You don't deserve it." You bet your ass I still deposited that check, but to this day I catch myself giving the "I worked the system" caveat whenever it comes up . . . like right here in this paragraph. I make excuses for my success, even though I worked long and hard to earn that cash.

Buying my first apartment was another milestone. I had never once lived in place that wasn't a rental, and had never even lived without a roommate, so having a home that was actually mine—well, I can tell you there were tears when I signed those closing documents. Creating that kind of safety net was some emotional shit, but I didn't enjoy it as much as I should have—there was that voice again, warning me that if I got too comfortable, if I celebrated too much, the universe would have the last laugh. The Lord giveth and the Lord taketh away. Something like that.

And yet, so far, the floor hasn't fallen out from under me. I have not been "found out." It turns out this pretty face might just deserve all the success that has come his way. And when I can't bring myself to believe that, I remind myself to be my own hype man. It's a good antidote to imposter syndrome, as weird as it feels in the moment. Talk to yourself out loud and say the things you need to hear: "I'm proud of myself." "I've made it." "Holy shit, I just did that." It might feel awkward—it still does for me sometimes—but it helps create a habit of celebrating your success. Learning to believe your own worth is a process, and it starts with hearing the message.

In fact, let me offer you my three-step plan to believing your own hype. Step one: Hear the message. Take it in. Don't shrink away or push back or make excuses. Just hear whatever it is you're saying. Step two: Feel whatever emotions come with that message. Discomfort, maybe (ask yourself, why?), but also hopefully joy and pride. Don't pass judgment on those feelings or assign them any value. Feeling proud of yourself is not cocky. Enjoying your success is not greed. It's okay to be happy! It's great to be proud! But it's also okay if hearing positive messages about yourself makes you feel guilty or embarrassed. There are no good or bad feelings, only feelings you need to investigate. Number three: Once you've heard the message and felt the message, only then can you begin to believe the message. That's a hard step. It involves clearing mental roadblocks, which is never easy, but it's transformative when you get there. So start by celebrating yourself, out loud. When you say it enough, and you hear it enough, I promise you'll begin to believe your own hype. As well you should.

None of this will happen overnight. Knowing your value takes work and time. And while I usually promote patience, rules are made to be broken. This time I say, fake it till you make it. No matter how you feel deep down, I want you to go out into the world as if you deserve everything that's coming to you and then some. Confidence! Assertiveness! Fearlessness! Every time you question yourself, I want you to say to yourself, *The fee is going up.* Repeat after me: THE FEE IS GOING UP. Ask for a raise. Charge more for your service. You have worked hard, you have invested your time, you have given a lot of yourself, and it's time to reap the benefits. You know what you have to offer. You know your skill set. You know where you excel. Now go get paid accordingly.

As you face the world with *The fee is going up* energy, remember that it's not only about money. *The fee is going up* is a mindset. It's about valuing yourself in every space and knowing that your time is precious. If you're working out, if you're investing in a friendship, if you're baking loaves of sourdough like the pandemic queen you are . . . whatever you give your time to, I want you to expect more in return.

And here's the thing about raising your fee: Once you see that people will pay you more for the same work, you won't be so willing to settle for less than you deserve. Just as being poor motivated me to hustle hard and pull myself up, making bank and enjoying luxuries motivates me to stay at that level. Steve Harvey had this viral clip where he talks about flying first-class. He basically says that everyone should fly first-class one time, because once you know what it feels like—the wide seats, the hot nuts, the washcloth, the drinks—it's very hard to walk past those seats the next time you board a flight. You'll always look for opportunities to make more money, because you won't want to go back to coach. Steve Harvey's out here dropping bombs, and he's absolutely right. Having money is nearly as powerful a motivator as not having it—once you've experienced the joy of success, you want to keep it going. You want to sustain whatever lifestyle you've become passionate about.

I know Steve Harvey was speaking metaphorically, but if there's one thing I've become bougie about in the last few years, it's travel. Not hotels, mind you; I'd rather stay in an Airbnb that feels like the local culture than pay for a four-star hotel. But I almost always fly first-class. That leg room? That cocktail?! Steve knows what he's talking about. And listen, I'm not a total diva. When I came back from Coachella recently I had to fly coach—it was fine. I did it. But I've become accustomed to the superior flight experience, and that's a perk of all this hard work. So yes, 95 percent of the time if you catch me on a flight, I will be sitting up front.

That doesn't mean I spend with abandon. I'm not going to pick the pricier option just because I can. I've got it, but that doesn't mean I flaunt it. People are always surprised these days to hear that I take the subway. It's cheaper and faster and I'm going to get where I'm going with less stress than if I'd taken a car. I'll always choose comfort and convenience over spending for the sake of spending. Most of the time I feel out of place in super-refined old-school money spaces. Yes, I have similar coin to you, but you people are boring. You're lame! Your whole personality is having money, and sorry if I'd rather be with the fun kids than the uber-rich fogeys with nothing interesting to say. It's like

Fire Island gays versus Hamptons gays. Fire Island gays are fun and rambunctious and just here to have a good time. They have money and spend money, but their money is not the star of the show. *They* are the star of the show. When you go to the Hamptons, everything revolves around cash and status and who has the biggest parties. It's a giant performance to prove that you belong.

I, dear reader, am, and always will be, a loud and proud Fire Island gay.

CHAPTER SIXTEEN

Let It Go, Elsa

In the fall of 2018, I went on a weeklong silent meditation retreat in Suquamish, Washington. I'd started meditating after my breakup with Matheus, and now I was working toward becoming a certified coach. A silent retreat was the final requirement, so there I was, sleeping in a janky bed in a Christian camp dorm room, sharing a bathroom with a seventy-year-old man whose name I never even learned. Every day was the same: five A.M. wake up, meditate, go to breakfast, meditate, go to lunch. Then there was some free time, during which I would work out with no equipment before meditating some more, having dinner, and going to sleep. There was no talking, no phones, no TV, no reading. Anything that could serve as a distraction from your thoughts was strictly verboten. (I cheated a little, I confess. I didn't use my phone for internet or to talk to anyone, but I did look at old photos. Any time I'm on a plane or somewhere with no service, I scroll through old memories. There's something very comforting about it.)

Doing nothing might not sound all that hard—for a workhorse like me, you'd think it'd be a welcome break— but, fuck, that week put me through the wringer. There I was, sitting with my own thoughts, day after day. I was disconnected from everything that kept me busy. There was no hiding from the endless scroll of anxieties or emotions or traumas that I'd spent so long burying and ignoring. By day five of a week like that, shit gets really trippy. I'd sit outside, immersed in the nature of the Pacific Northwest, and think about all the different ecosystems at work. The birds were calling to one another in their own bird language, the ants were working together in their little ant colonies. Each of these worlds relied on interdependence—it wasn't just me that had to count on others to survive; literally every living being is here thanks to another living being. The intricacies of life, and the fact that any of these communities actually thrive, was blowing my mind. I'm telling you, it was like being really high without the drugs.

By the end of the week I thought I was a fucking Jedi. You could not convince me otherwise. *I see the Force, bitch.* It was challenging as all hell, but it was also one of the most rewarding weeks of my life. Talking to no one but yourself for seven days is pretty much a crash course in self-love. It's like a long and intimate first date, with plenty of time to ask yourself hard questions and no rush to get the answers. It's just you and your thoughts, finally getting to know each other. And turns out, when you cut through all the mental clutter, what really matters becomes quite clear. The answer is . . . drum roll, please . . . not that much. Other than being alive, giving love, and getting love back, the rest of the shit swirling in your orbit is truly not that deep.

As you come to the end of this book, boo, I hope that's what you remember. Because in some ways, self-love gets a bad rap. We talk about it in such a serious manner, always focused on doing The Work, but what we lose in those heady conversations is how much fun it can be to love ourselves, and to do so without apology. When you find yourself in a place where you can say, *This is who I am, a beautiful ho who will make mistakes but is doing her best,* it makes it a lot easier to laugh at yourself when you do weird shit. It's easier to shrug off mistakes and try again next time. You can recognize when you fall into old patterns, have a good laugh, forgive yourself, and move on. *Here I am, back on my bullshit.* When you know you're coming from a place of goodness, none of it seems that serious, because there's always next time.

Writing a book is a little bit like sitting through a very (very!) long therapy session. Every lesson I'm sharing with you also serves as a reminder to myself, because I don't always get it right. I've learned the hard way more than once. I cannot tell you how many times I've shown up at a Peloton class on a Friday or Saturday morning only to announce to the camera that I'm on the struggle bus. Sure, I could have stayed home the night before and gotten nine hours of sleep and eaten a sensible meal and drank only an eight-ounce glass of water. And sometimes I make that choice. But other times your girl wants to go out into the streets of New York City and be a slut. She wants to stay up too late and make bad decisions and deal with the repercussions later. Being a human in the world can be messy and difficult, and we've earned the right to let our hair down and get a little sloppy sometimes. So please, make as many mistakes as you need to. You're human, you're flawed, mistakes happen. When you behave in ways that are misaligned with your intentions, I want you to vow to do better next time. And then I need you to let it go.

I don't believe in regrets. Well, if you are murdering someone—yes. Regret that. But otherwise, I say forgive yourself, make a plan for next time, and move on. Let it go, Elsa. I don't cancel anyone. We all do dumb shit. We all have moments of ignorance. If I've been a broken record about anything over these sixteen chapters, I hope it's the importance of giving yourself grace. When we fuck up, when we hurt other people . . . we can replay the tape over and over and beat ourselves up, or we can forgive ourselves and try to do better next time.

Mistakes, I'm here to tell you, are not the roadblock between you and your best self. Getting something wrong won't keep you from living the life you deserve. Playing it safe, that's the real problem. When we're too rigid about getting something "right," we forget to live our lives. So I want you to think long and hard about what's standing in your way. Is it you? Then move, bitch! Get out the way! Protecting yourself from sadness isn't really protecting yourself at all. Failure is the shake-up that knocks us off our path and lands us on a better one. There are so many times when my life didn't turn out as I'd hoped, and as I think back on each instance, my overwhelming sentiment is, *Thank God.* When I was a young teenager grappling with sexual confusion, all I wanted was to live a "normal" heterosexual life. I really didn't want to be gay. Now I can't imagine not being gay! If I had the choice right now to be gay or straight, I would always choose gay—I love that I've been able to experience life though this lens. I love being a part of this culture and community. And my dance ca-reer . . . all I wanted was to go on tour with this artist or that one. Thank the lord that didn't happen, because failing at dance is what put me on the path to Peloton. Can I get an amen?!

So let's not take it all so seriously, okay? Life is a joke, and guess what? You're in on it! Every moment is an op-portunity to grow, an opportunity to laugh, and an oppor-tunity to try something new. And yes, new things are scary. But until you show up and trust yourself and do the work, it's not going to get any easier. So do the scary thing. Take the leap. Go find your light.

Bye, boo.

Acknowledgments

As they say, gratitude is the attitude. I've also been told it takes a village to raise a child. So I'd like to spend a moment and give thanks to all of those who have raised this man-child. First and foremost I'd like to thank my mom, Cindy Rigsby. Thanks for loving me imperfectly, but the best that you could. Without all this childhood trauma, I would barely have a book to write.

I came into this world as an only child, but the world has gifted me Quintin Darnell Payton, who is not only the closest thing I have to a sibling but is my forever platonic life partner.

Fourteen-plus years in New York City have given me an incredible chosen family. Unfortunately, not all of those family members will be able to read the words on these pages. My dear Oscar, I miss you every day. Thank you for a uniquely purposeful friendship. I know you would be proud of this accomplishment.

Every chosen family has its ups and downs, and I'm so lucky to have a group of gworls to experience this chaotic dance we call life with. Andrew Chappelle, thanks for the ATV ride through the picturesque hills of Mykonos. Every turn we took that day served as inspiration to my career in more ways than one. Cory Stewart, no one knows how to plan a Disney vacation quite like you. Always go left. Patrick Crough, I love you and I'm proud of you, boy. Patrick Pittles little-piece-of-skin Hartigan Darab, thank you for many years of friendship, letting me crash on your couch, and other people's couches. I'm immensely grateful for you. Justin Dawson, thanks for the beats, the constant commentary on pop music, and the never-ending political discourse. Juanita, *te amo mucho.* Thiago, *obrigado por uma amizade incrível, te amo muito.* Rebecca French, thanks for many Thanksgivings and many years living together. David Cassagnol, no stage, speaker, or platform is ready for your dance moves. Brian Hyland, I love you like you love drag queens and Madonna. Aaron, we almost lost it all, but bitch, I'm proud of you.

Long before life gifted me a chosen family, I was given a real-life pretend sister. Kacie Ragland, I'm sorry for yelling at you in high school when we were doing our science project and you accused me of being gay. Turns out, you were right, bitch. I love you more than you love hoarding objects and Christmas. And to the woman that birthed you, Lynette, thanks for being another mom to me.

I have slept with more people than I can count, seriously dated a handful, but I've only really loved a few. Thank you to Matheus Cunha for the love that we experienced and for sharing your culture with me.

Andrés Eduardo Castello Alfaro, thank you for your support, your love, and choosing me.

Brett Ferguson, thank you for training me inside and

out, somehow that sounds sexual, but I mean it on a spiritual level.

To my team at A3, thanks for believing in me before the pandemic turned me into a marketable star. Alec Shankman, I'm sorry for playing hardball for such a long time, but hey, we made it. Thanks for all your guidance and help. And thank you for letting Adam Loria and Sydnie Rowland take such great care of me. Thank you to my literary agent, David Doerrer, and the rest of the team at A3. Thank you to Sara Weiss, Sydney Collins, and the entire team at Ballantine who helped put this book together: Kara Welsh, Jennifer Hershey, Kim Hovey, Debbie Aroff, Corina Diez, Emily Isayeff, Hope Hathcock, Richard Elman, Paolo Pepe, Ella Laytham, Andy Lefkowitz, Elizabeth Rendfleisch, Dan Novack. Thank you to my collaborator, Rachel Bertsche.

To Ren Anders, the younger sister I never asked for and never wanted, love ya, girly pop. Also, can you pick up my dry cleaning?

To the kings, queens, and royalty behind the scenes— thanks to Jen Cotter for clearing the path and letting me be me. To Amanda Hill and Emily Gaffney, thanks for keeping me and the entire production team organized. To John and Jill Foley, thank you. And thank you to Marion Roaman for seeing my potential and reminding me to stay humble no matter how big I get. Thank you to my boos and the entire Peloton community for laughing with me on this wild journey.

To all my fellow Peloton instructors, thanks for helping me through this unique journey. I'm incredibly proud of the community that we've built and to call you my teammates. To Jenn Sherman, thanks for the random phone calls, the chats in the dressing room, and always rooting me on. To Alex Toussaint, for always checking my vibe. To Robin Arzón, for inspiring me to be the best. To Jess King, for being my *hermana*. To Tunde Oyeneyin, for not giving up. To Matt Wilpers, for financial advice and an uncanny impression of me. To Hannah Marie Corbin, for being my personal Suze Orman. To Ally Love, whose birthday is an entire month. To Emma Lovewell, live, learn, and stop being so fucking good at everything.

Lastly, I'd like to thank myself, cuz if you can't thank yourself, how in the hell you gonna thank someone else?

ABOUT THE AUTHOR

Beloved fitness instructor CODY RIGSBY is a Peloton superstar. Rigsby is known for his witty humor, engaging storytelling, and pop culture hot takes as well as his insight into relationships and his advocacy for self-love. He was the second runner-up on the thirtieth season of *Dancing with the Stars*, and has cohosted the GLAAD Media Awards. Rigsby has been the face of numerous brands, including Adidas, Capital One, Chobani, Therabody, Chipotle, Gatorade, and more. He has been profiled in the *Los Angeles Times*, *People*, *The Washington Post*, *The New York Times*, *Vogue*, *GQ*, *Forbes*, *Vox*, *Us Weekly*, and *Time*, and on *Good Morning America*. Rigsby lives in Brooklyn, New York.